PICTURE BOOK OF

KITTENS

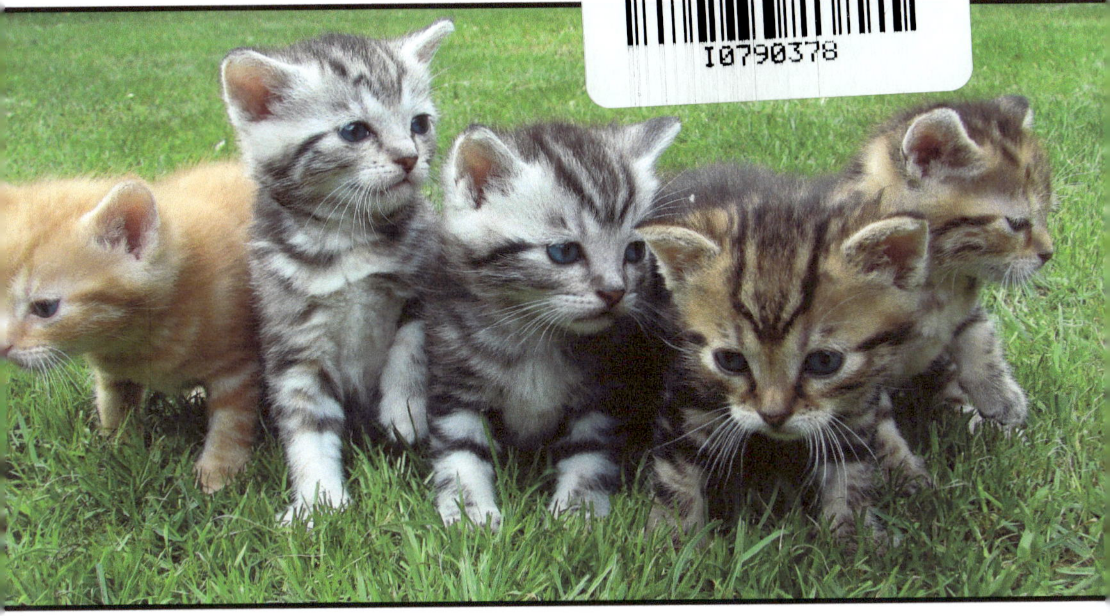

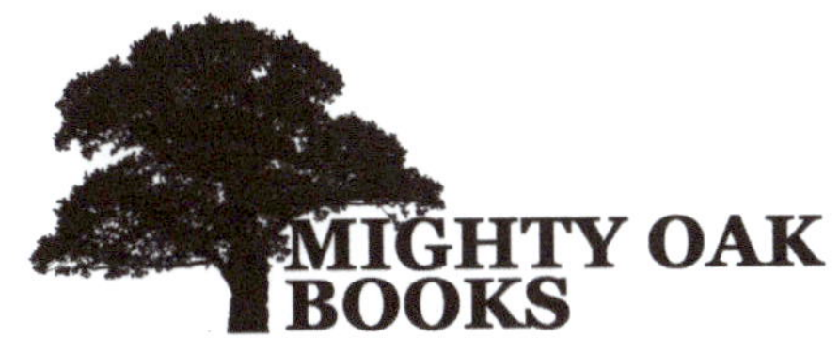

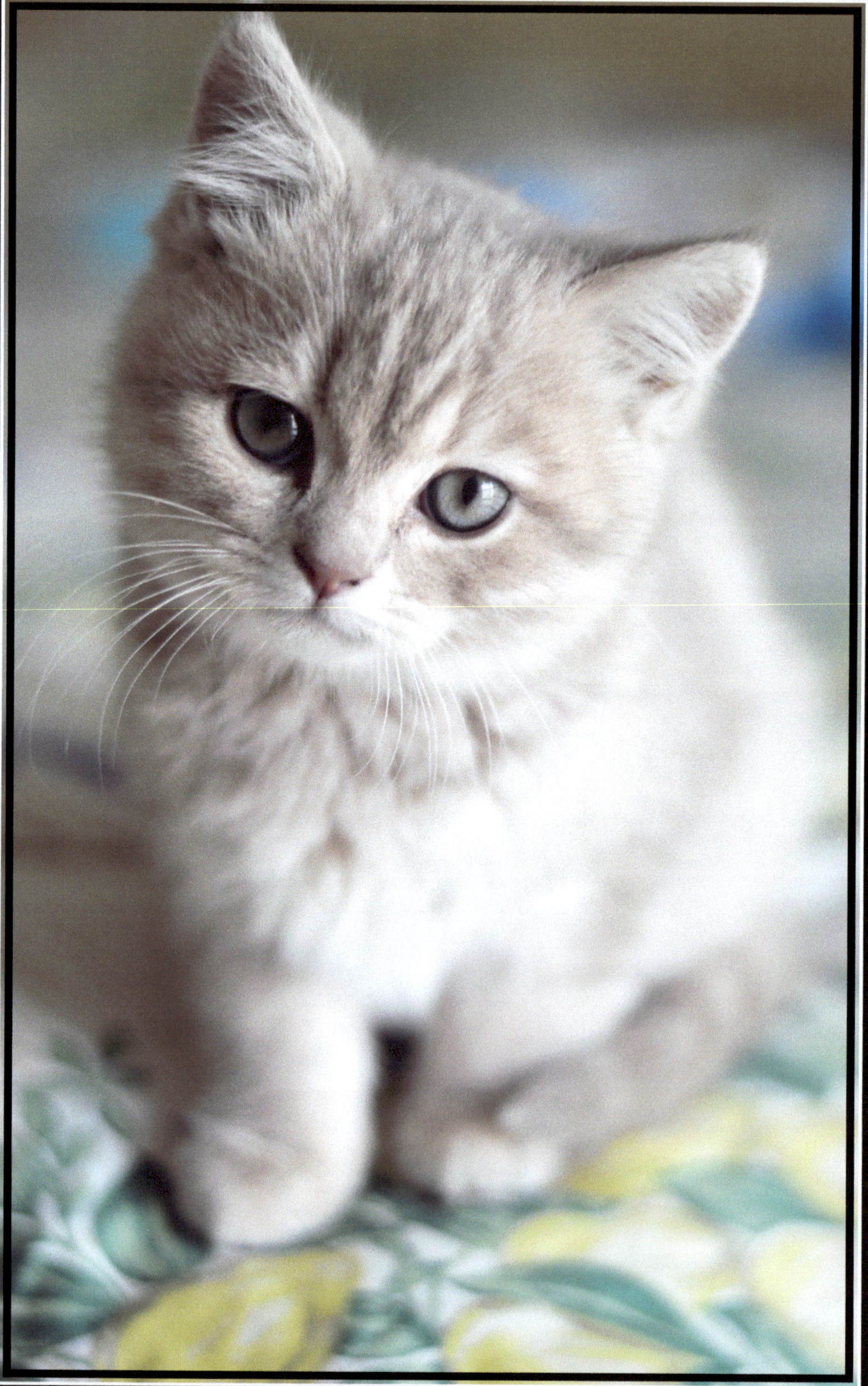

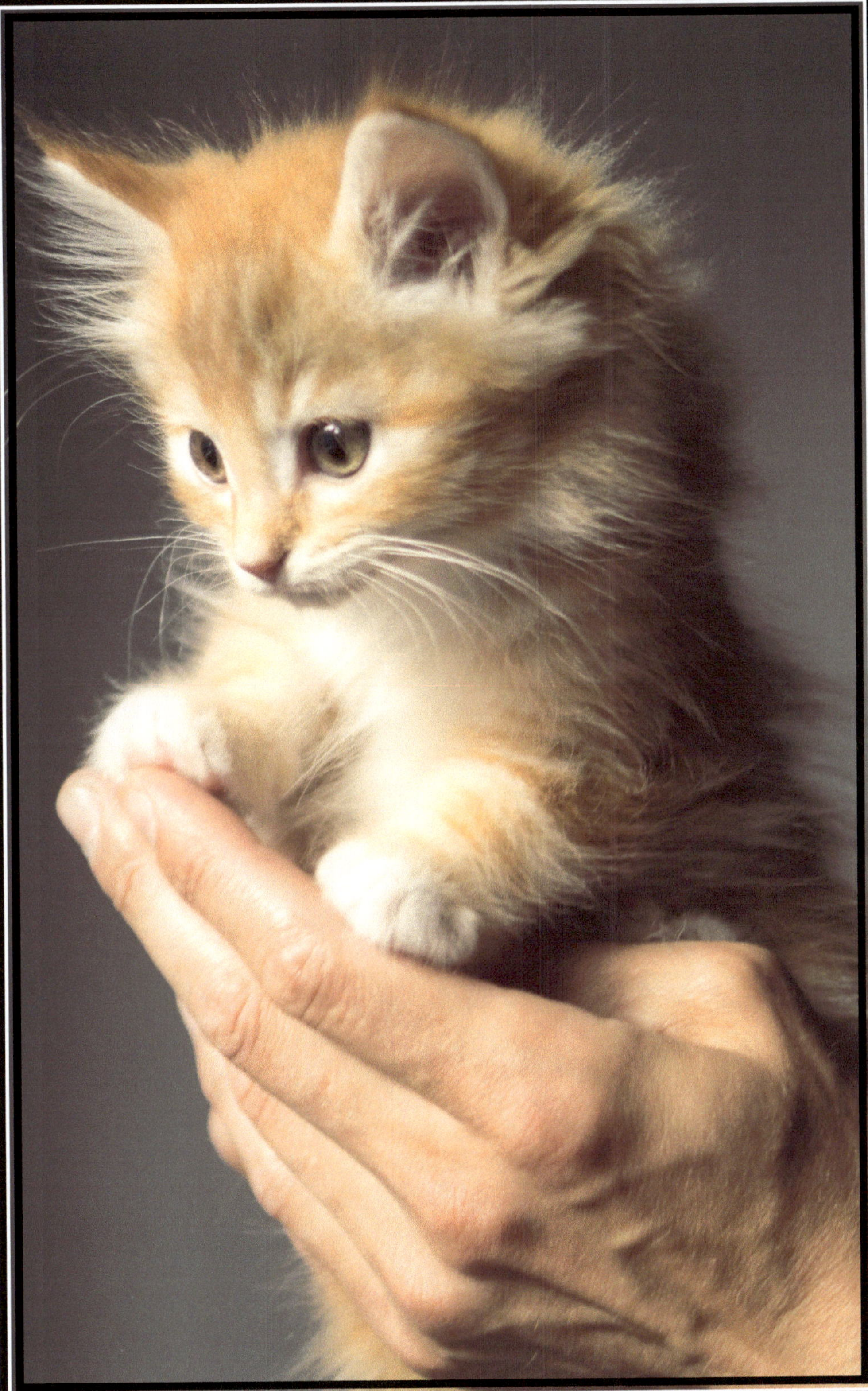

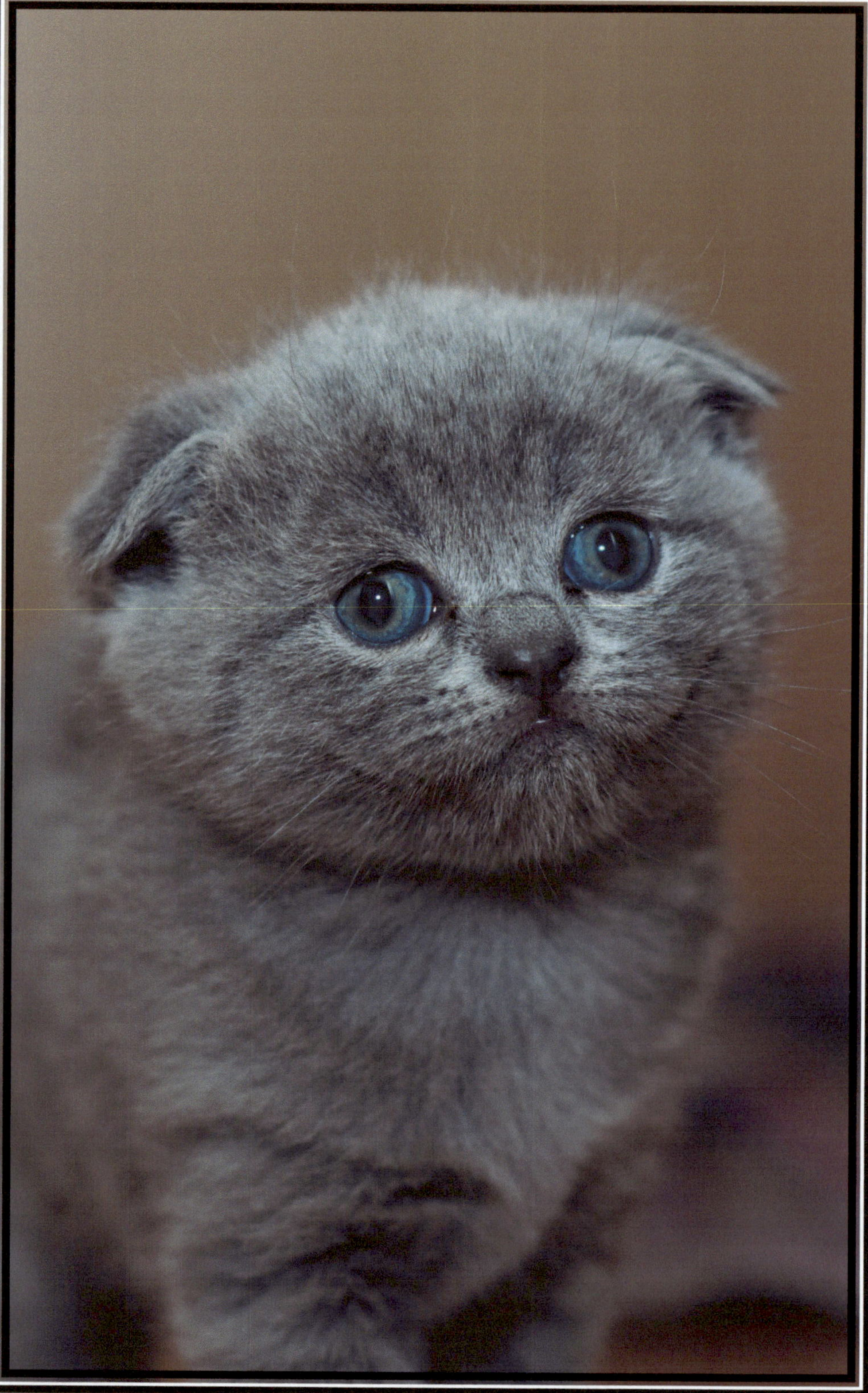

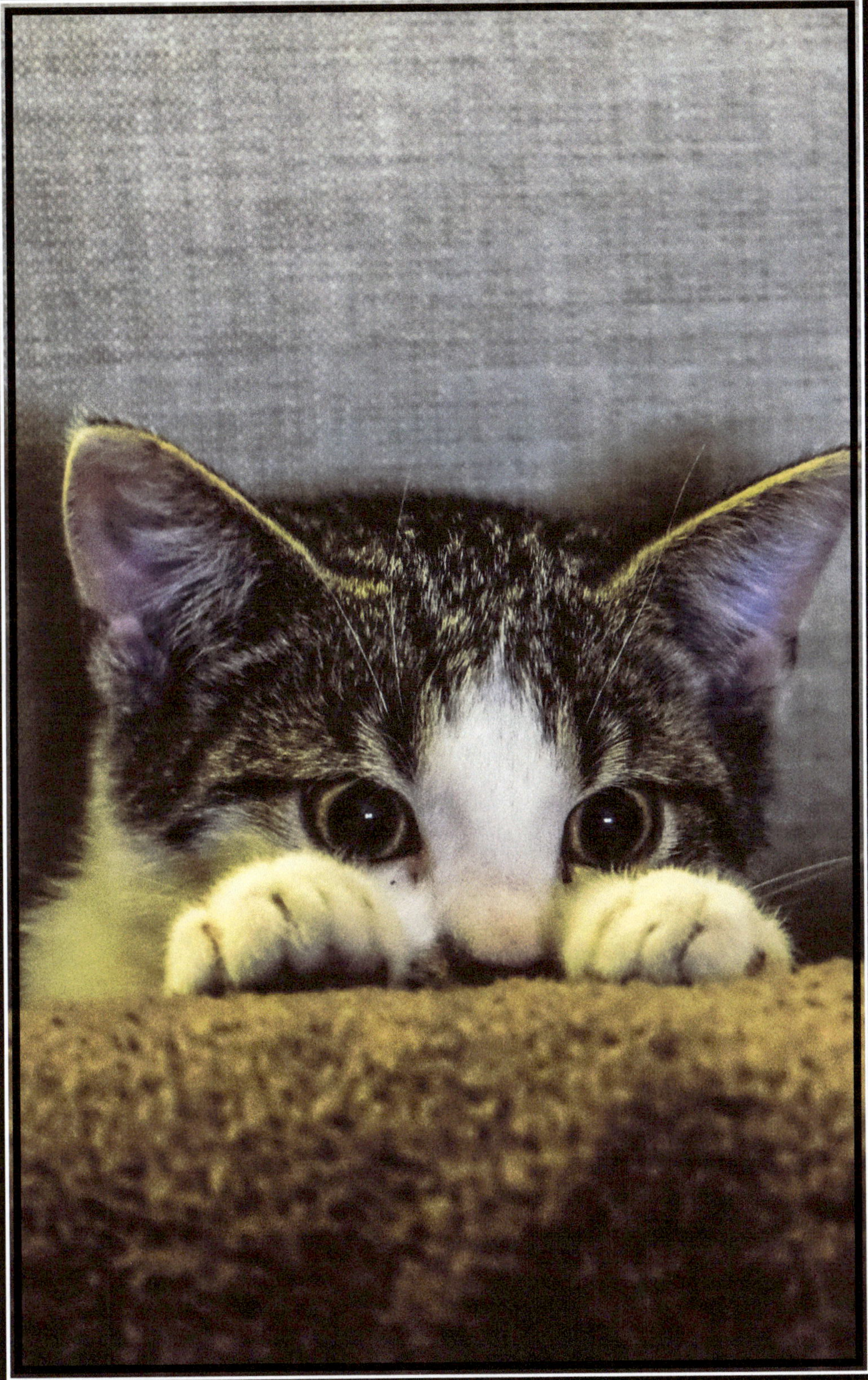

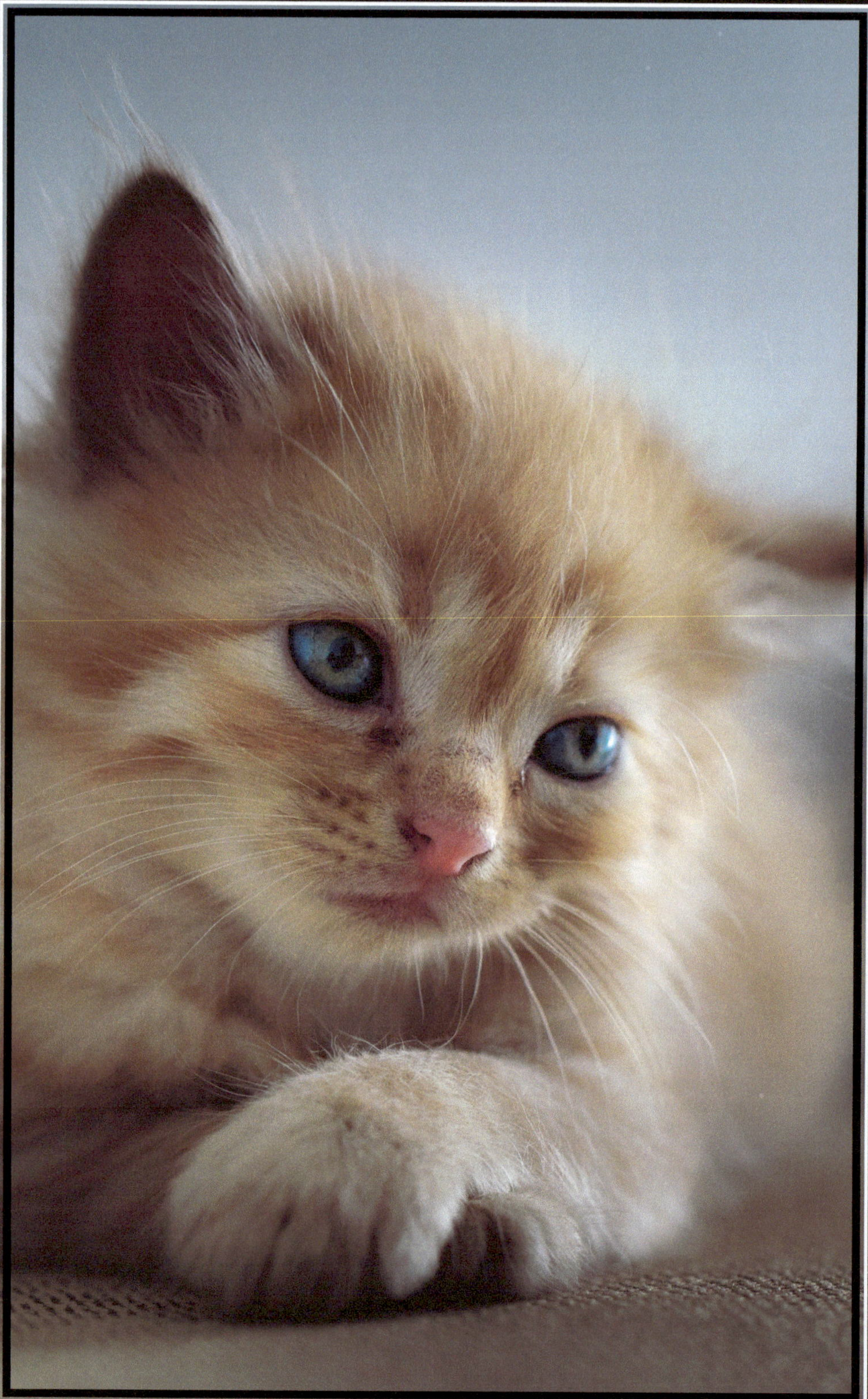

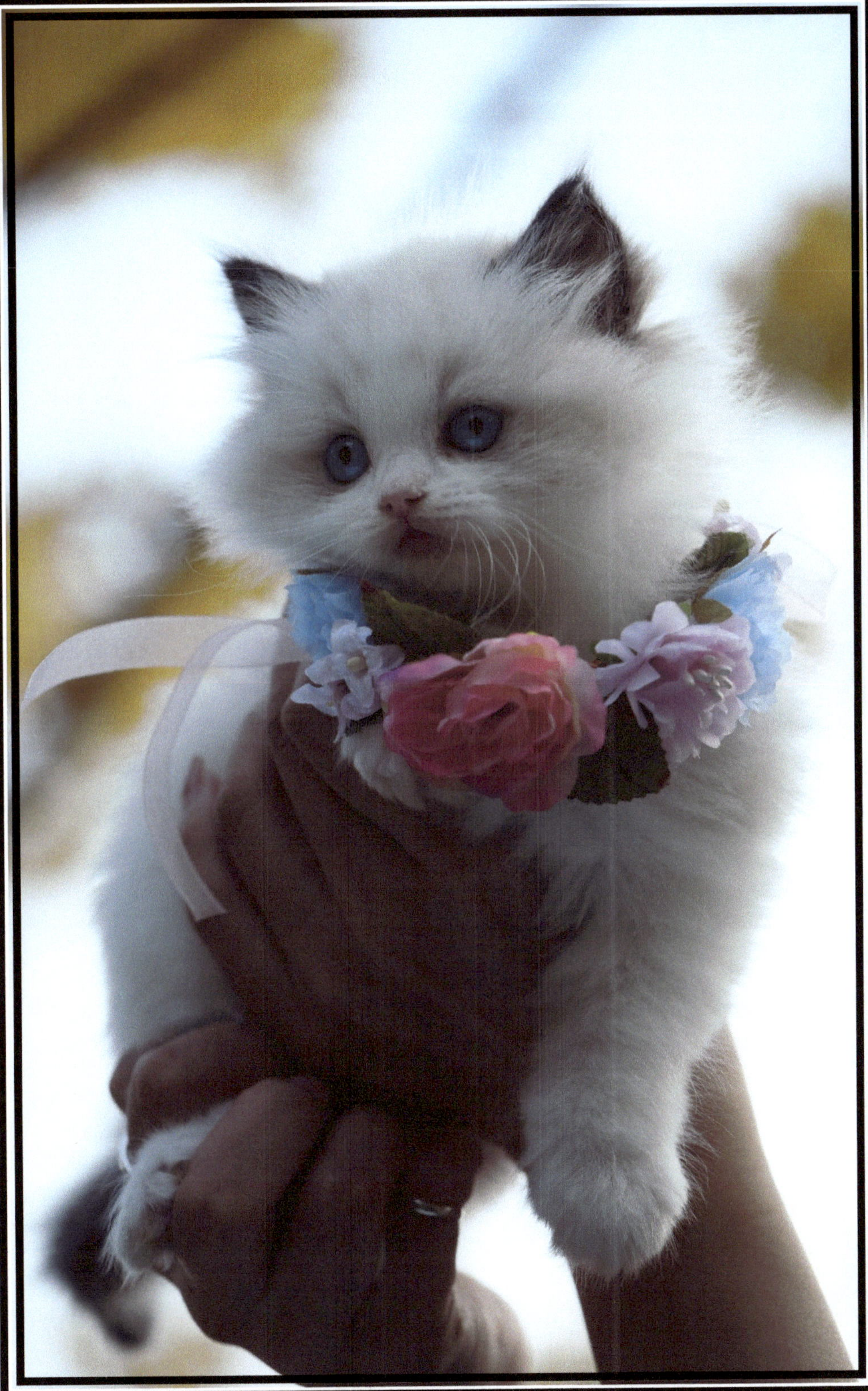

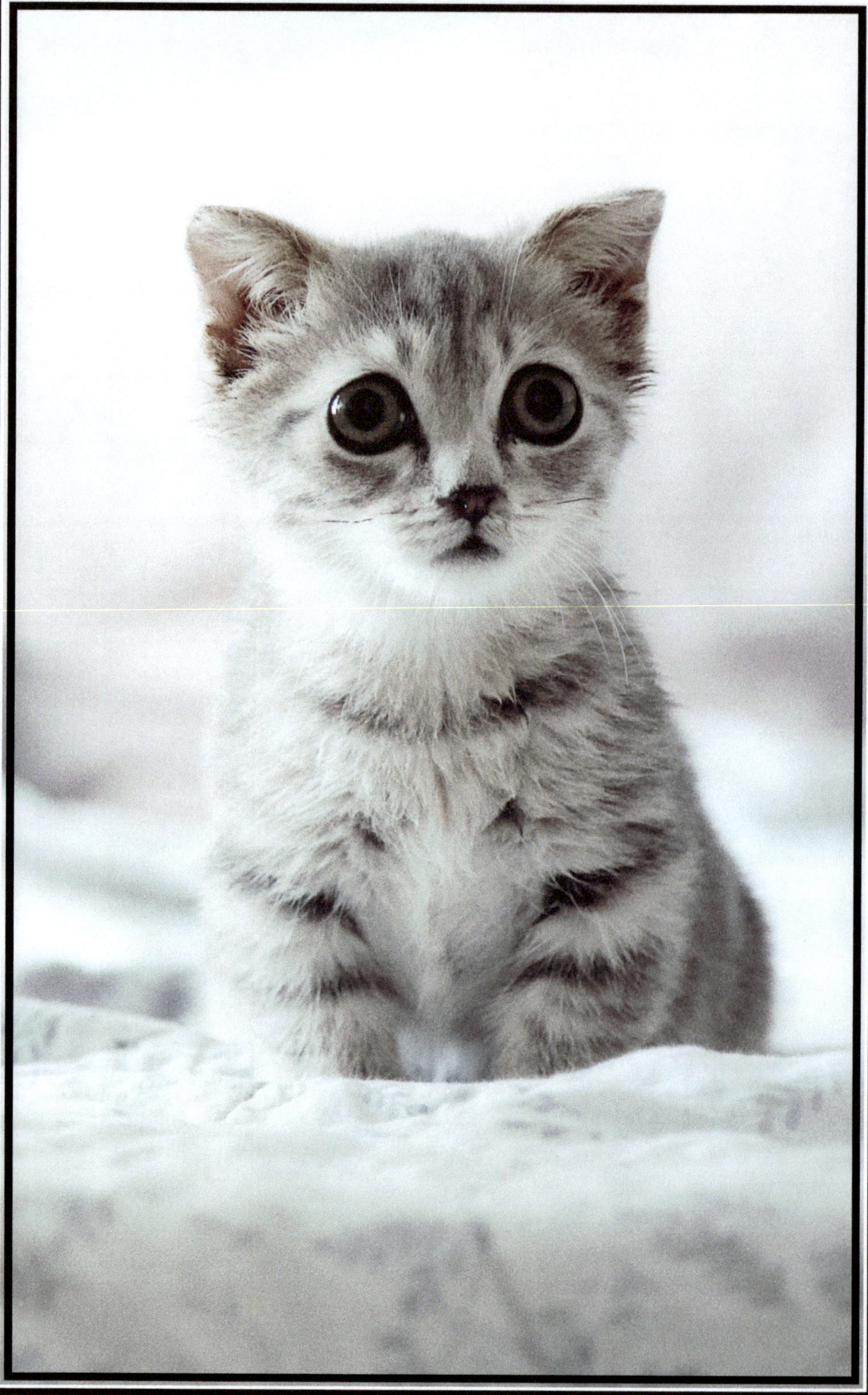

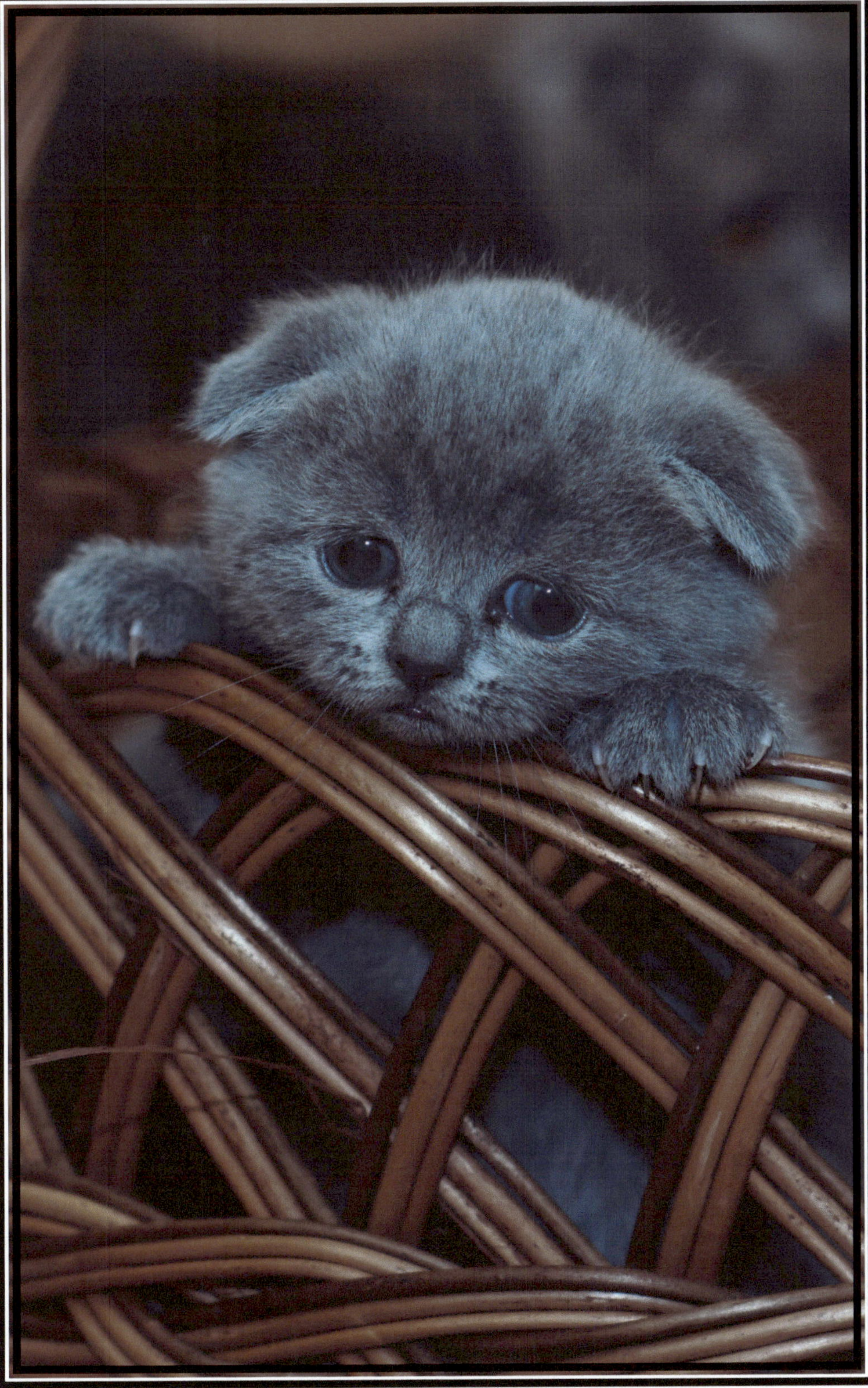

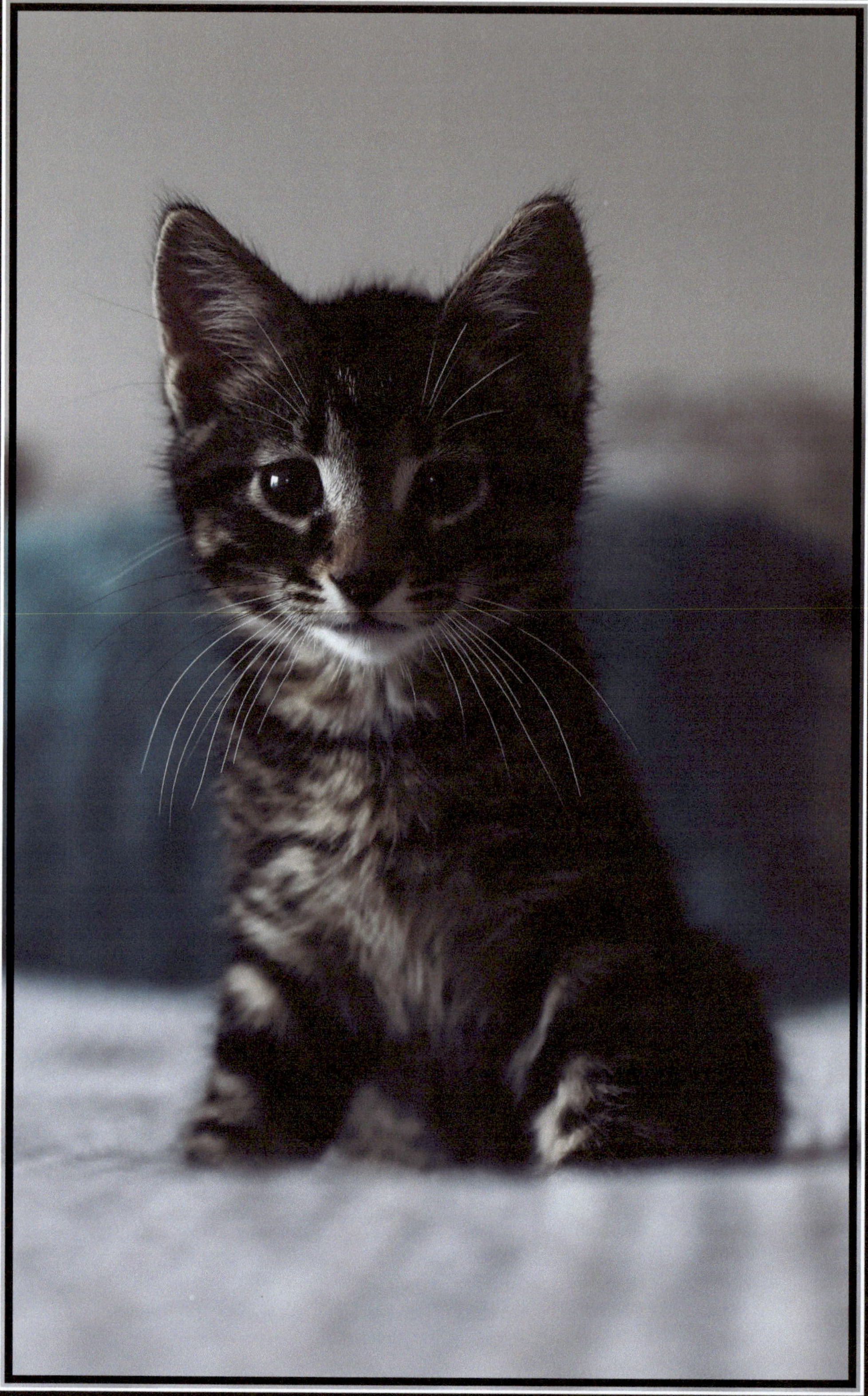

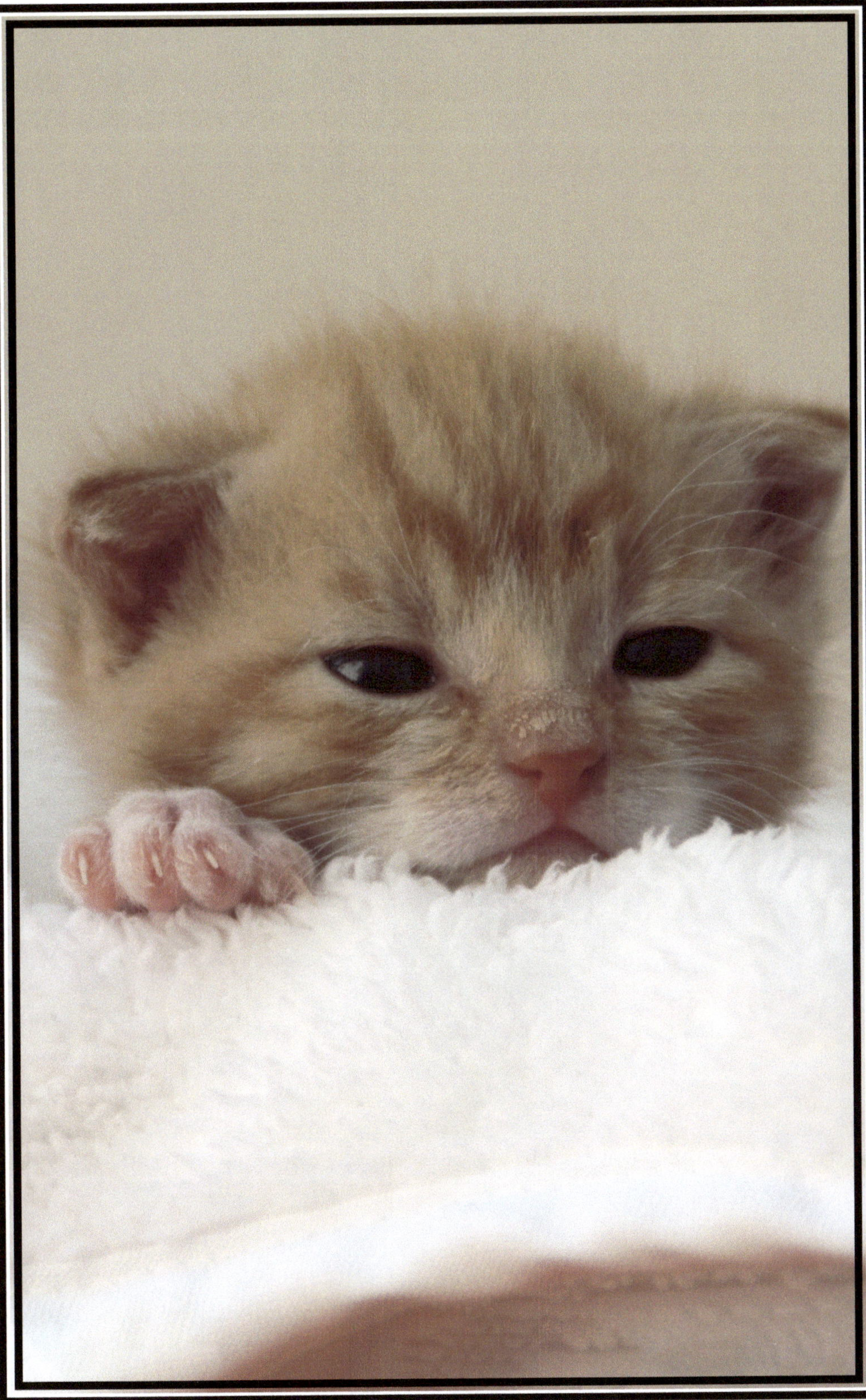

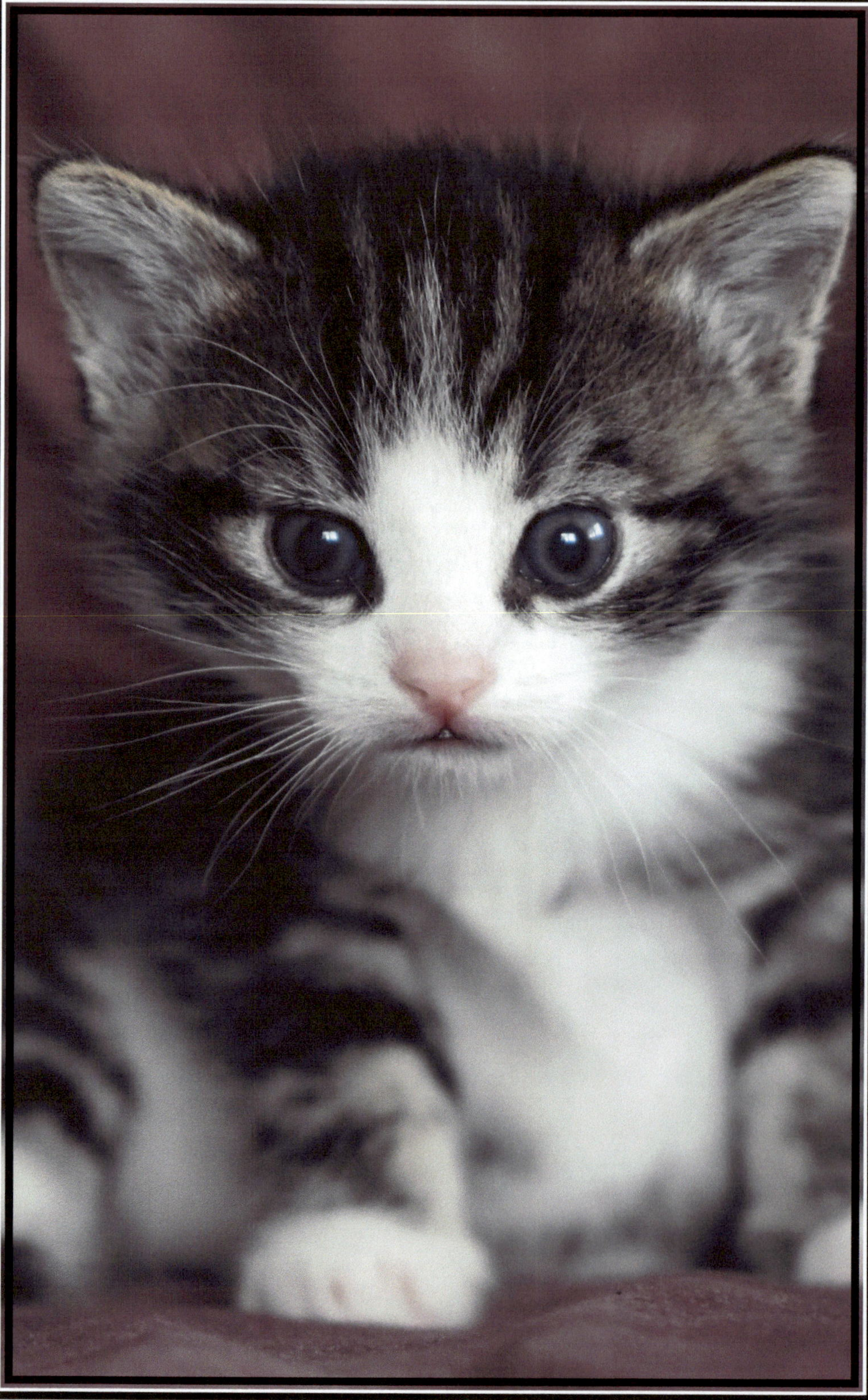

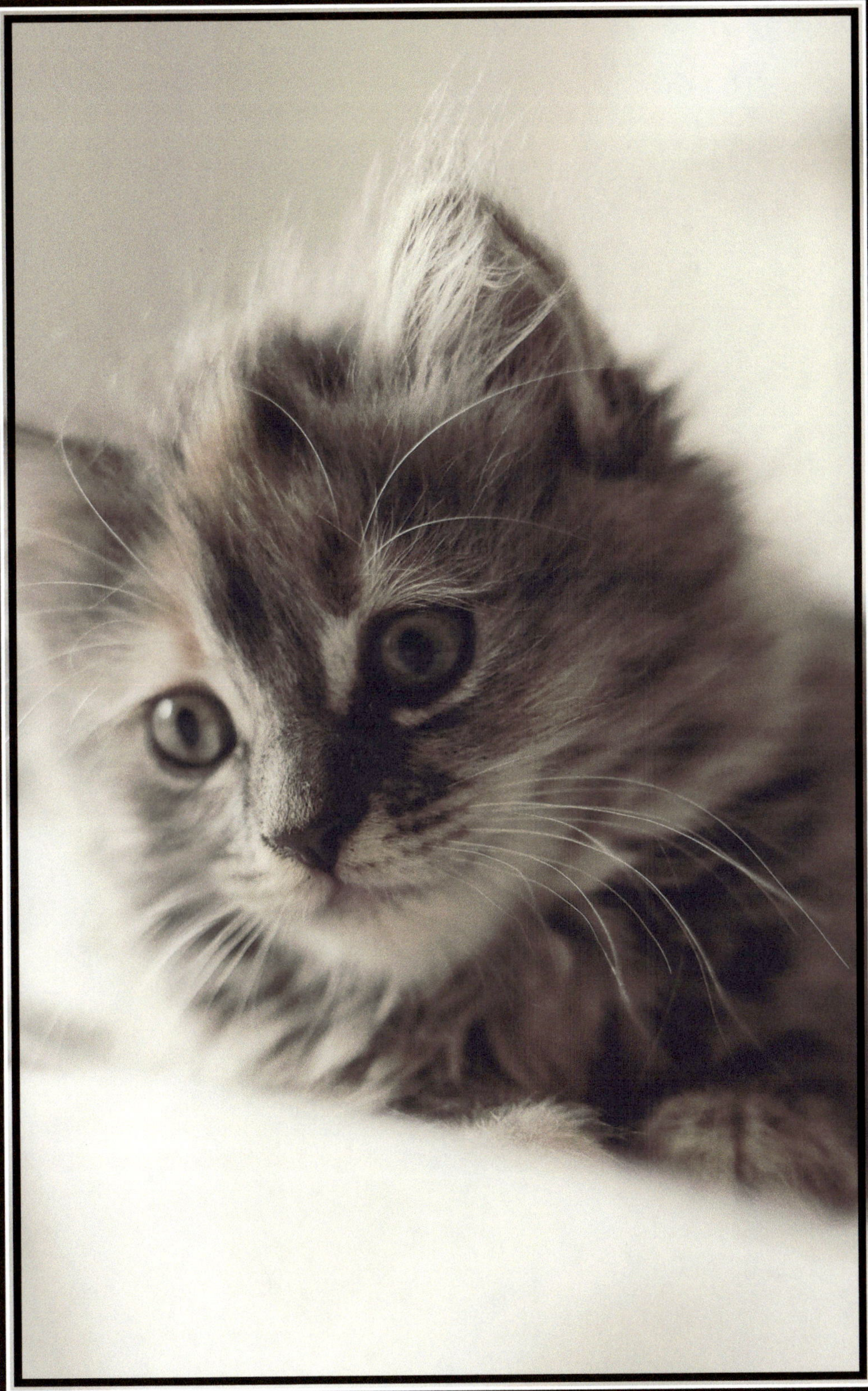

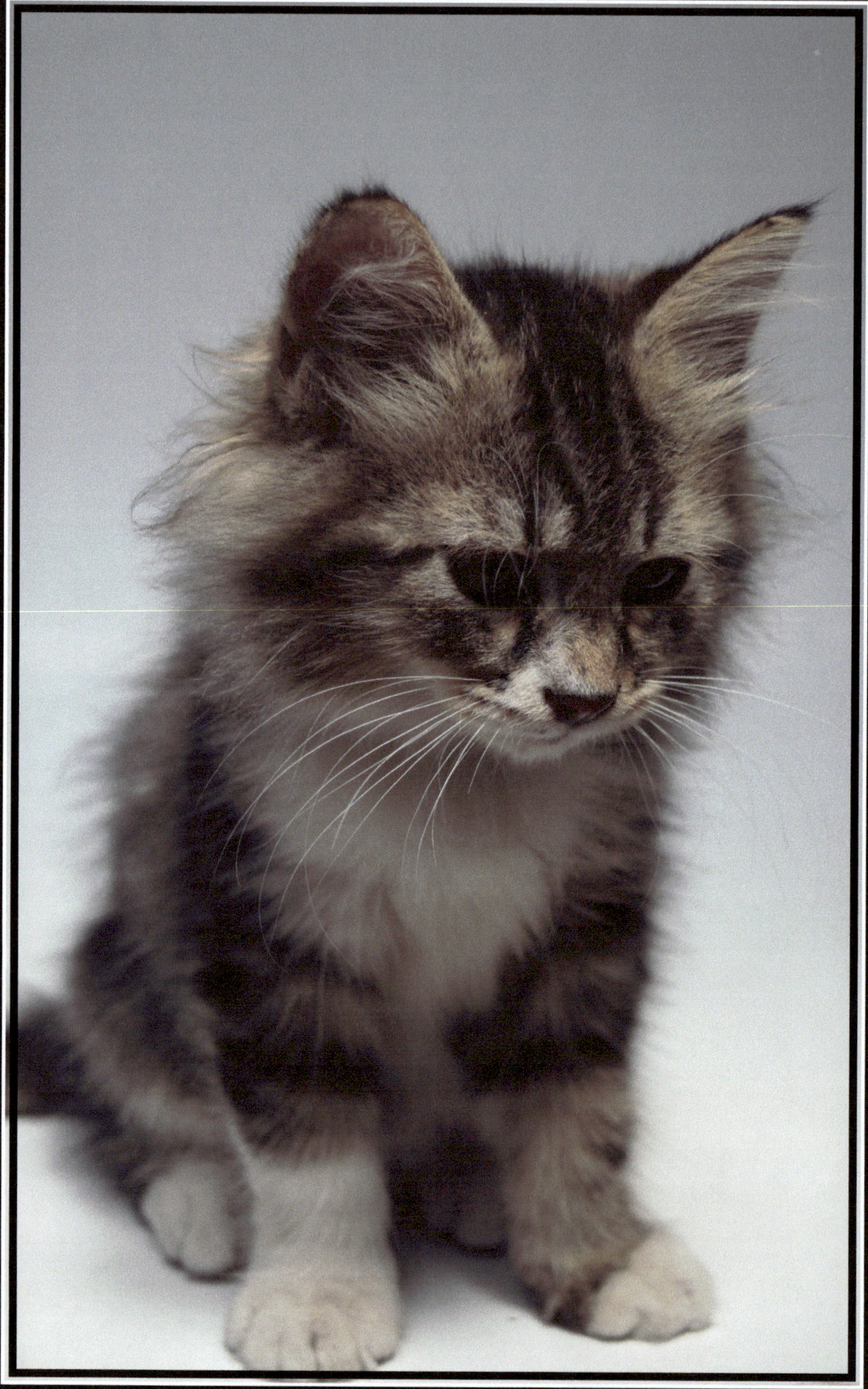

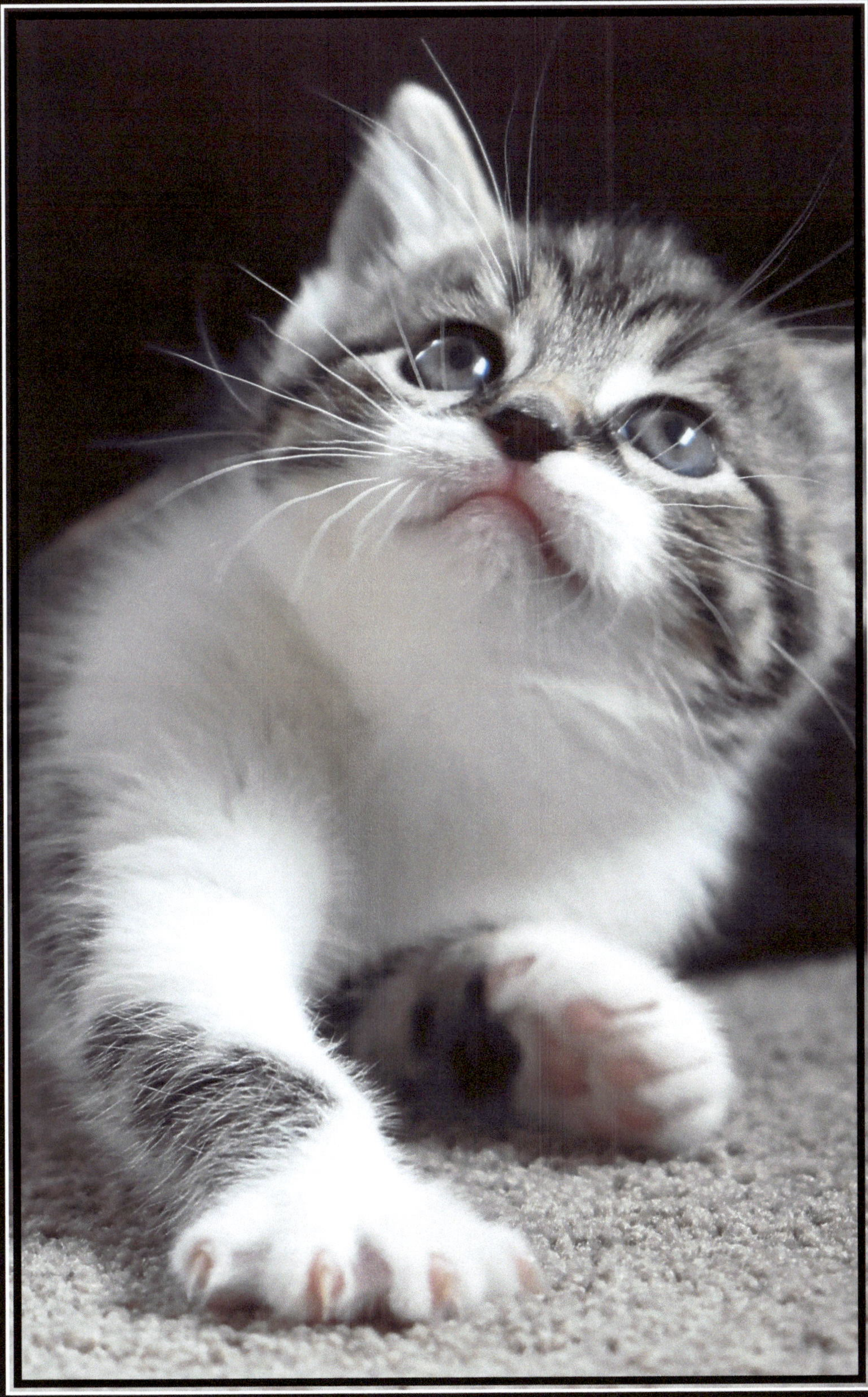

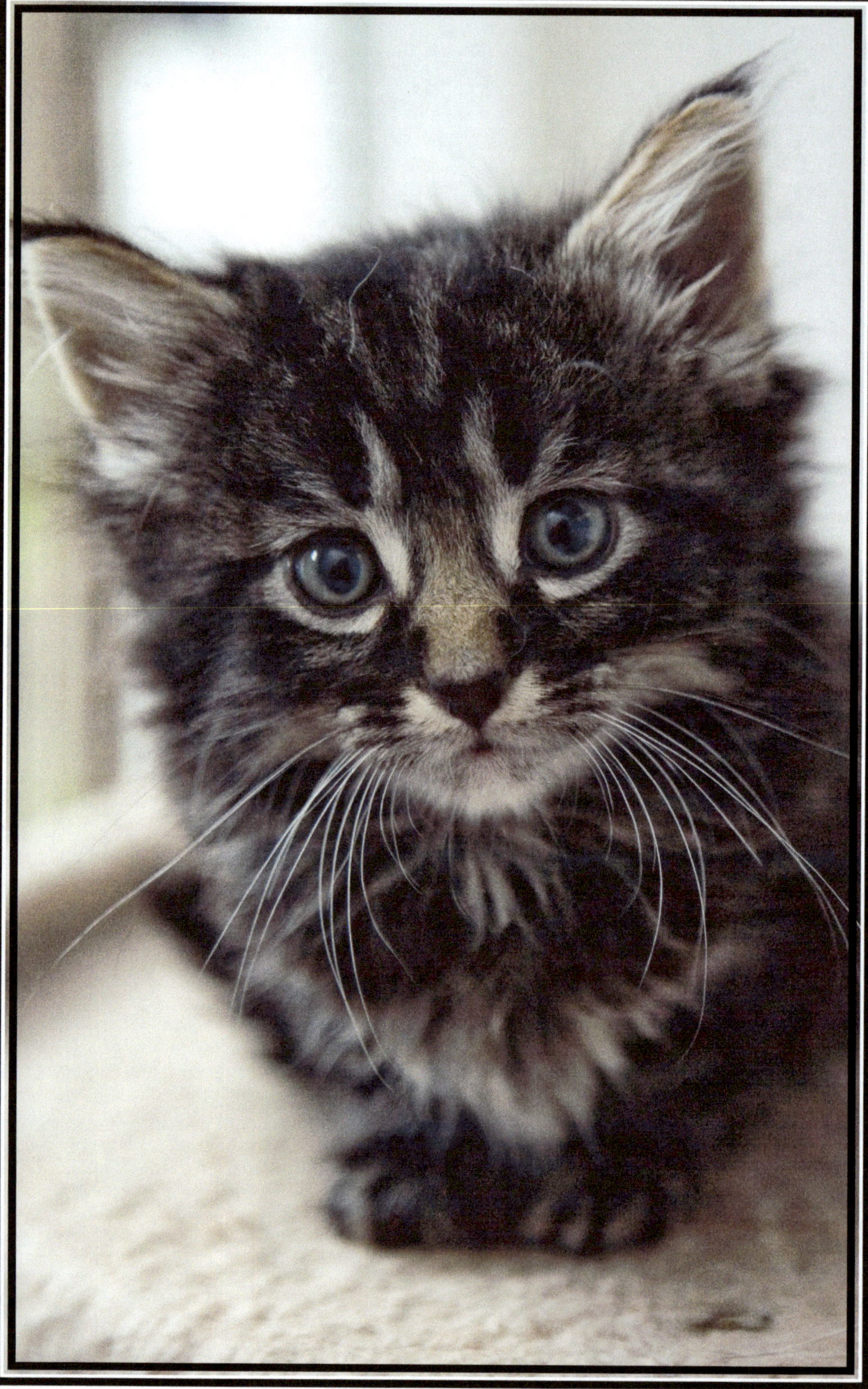

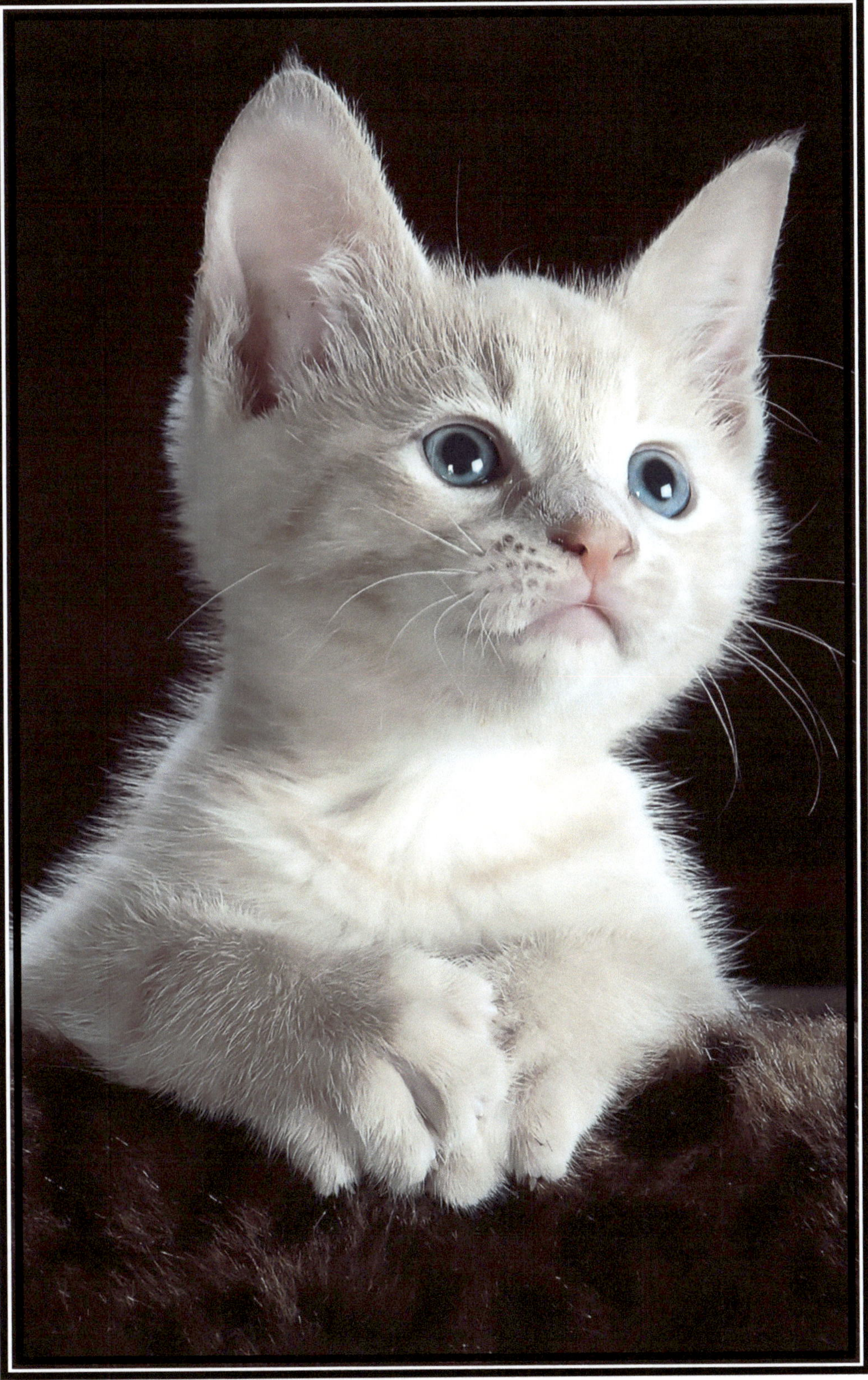

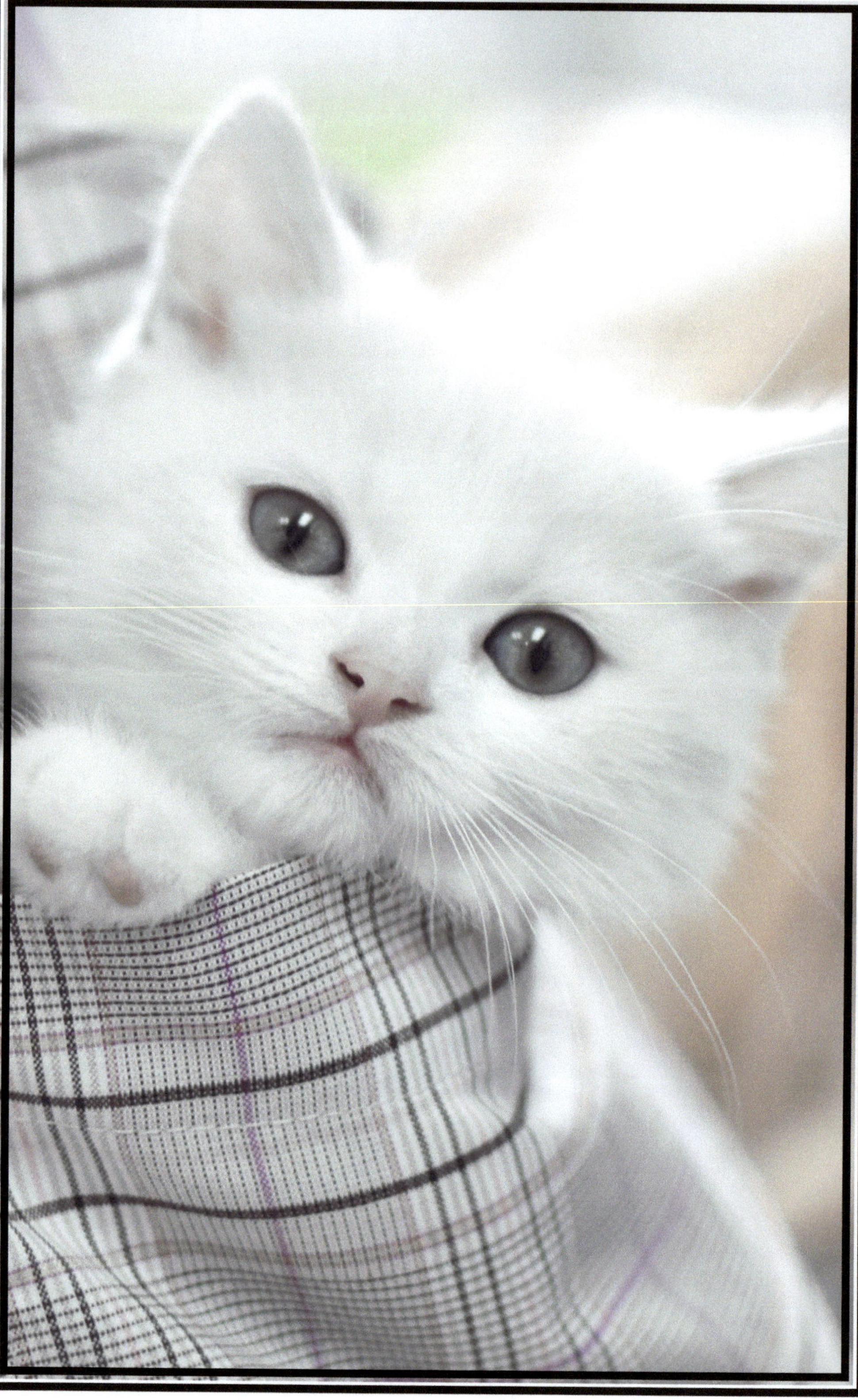

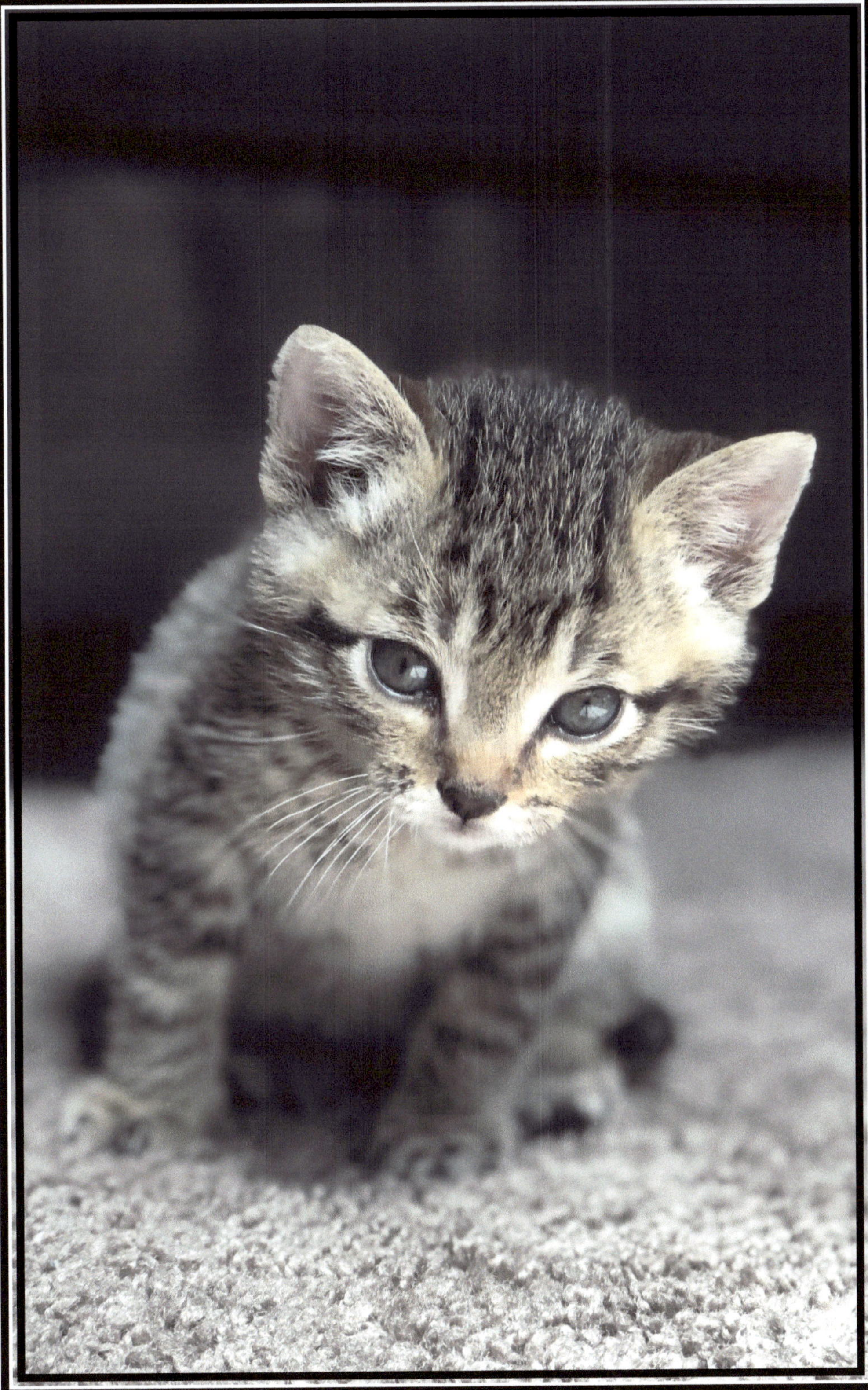

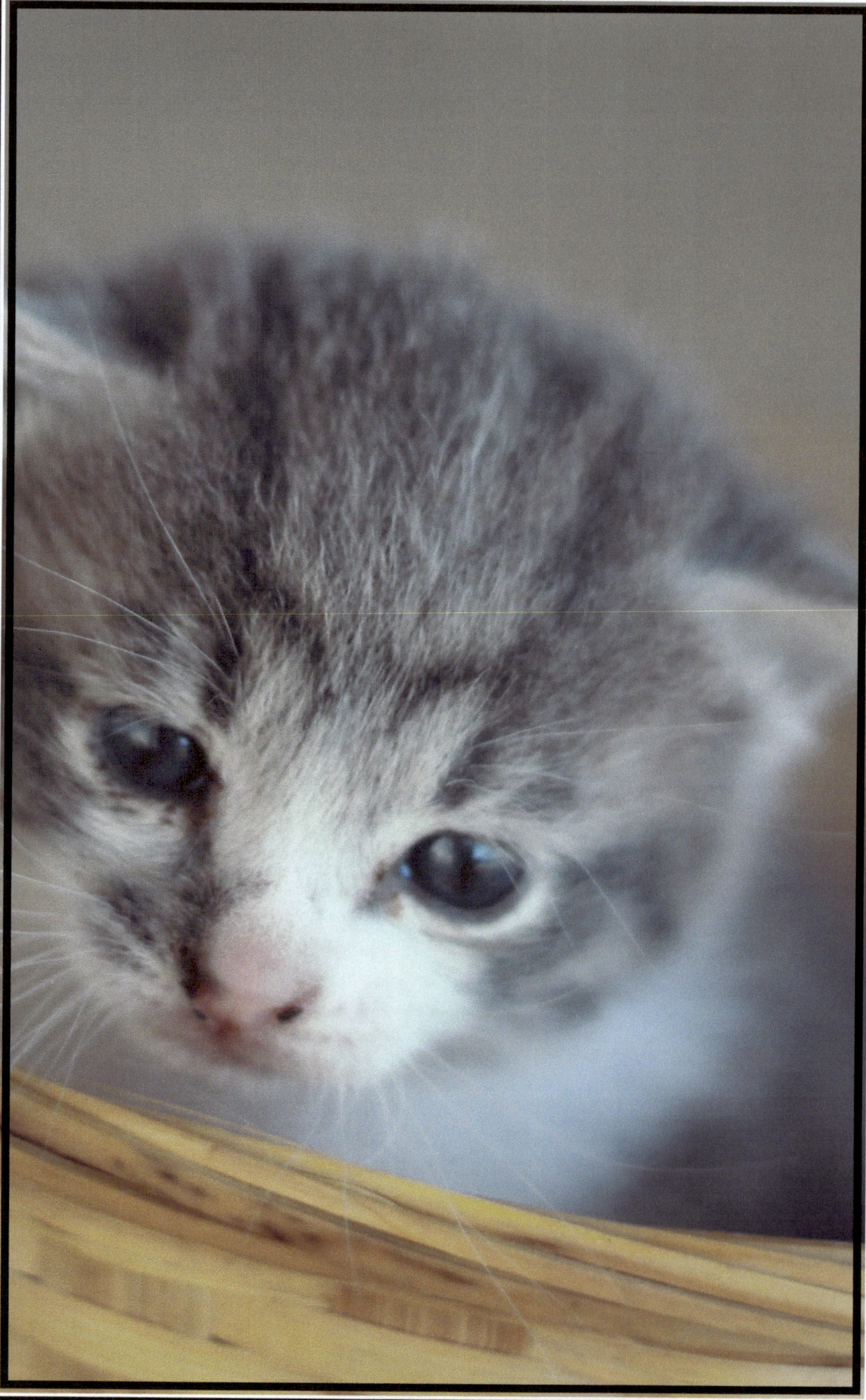

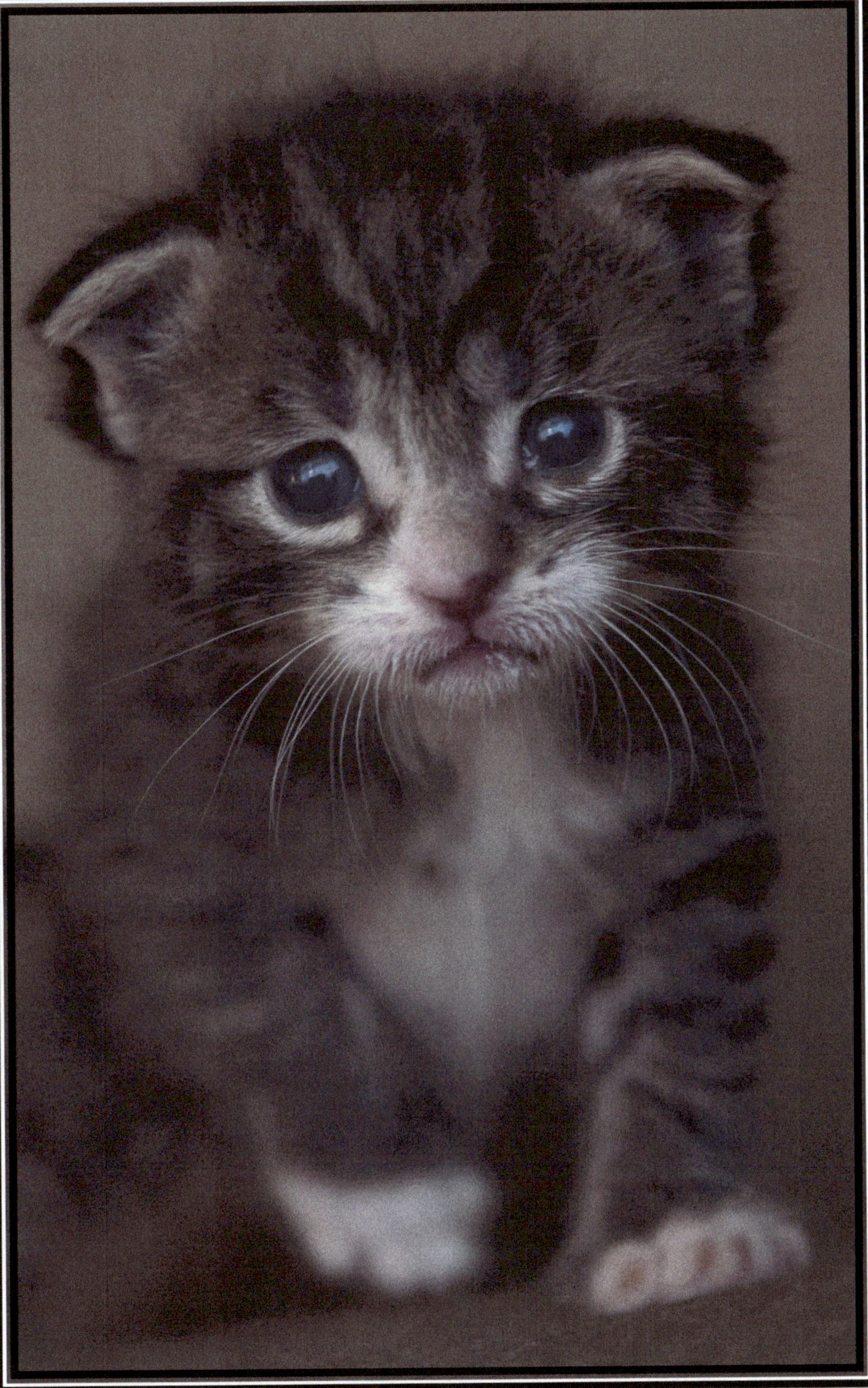

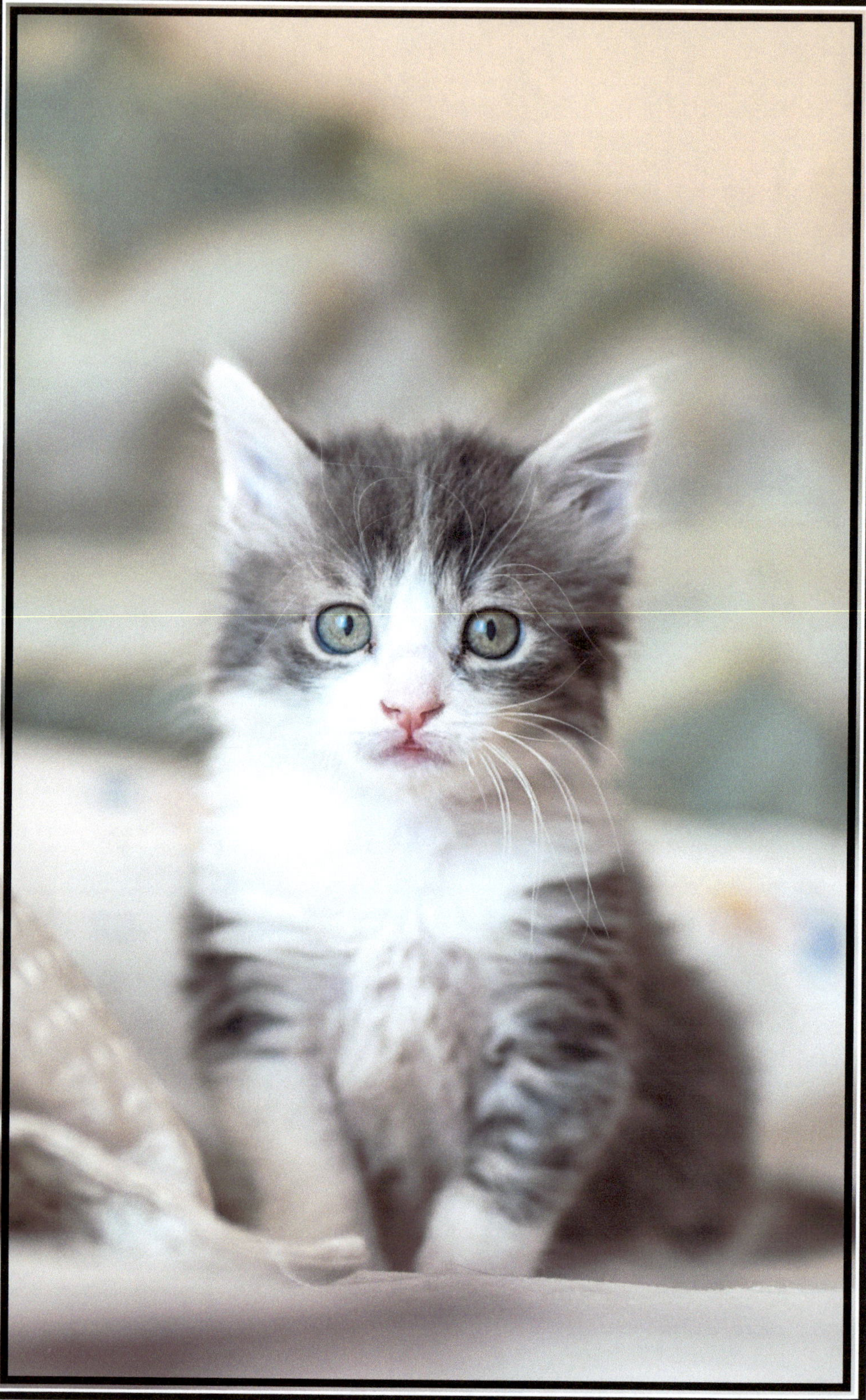

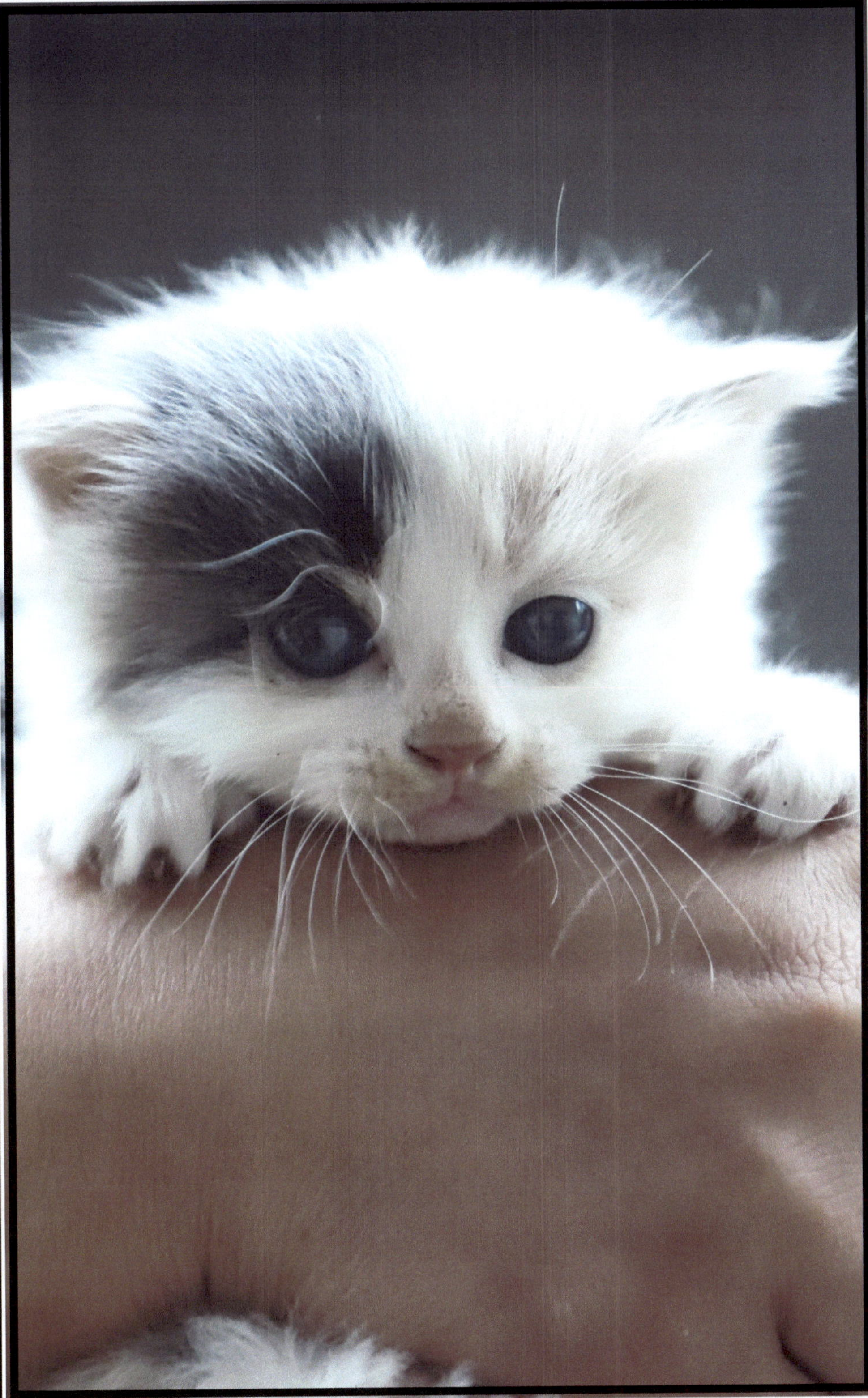

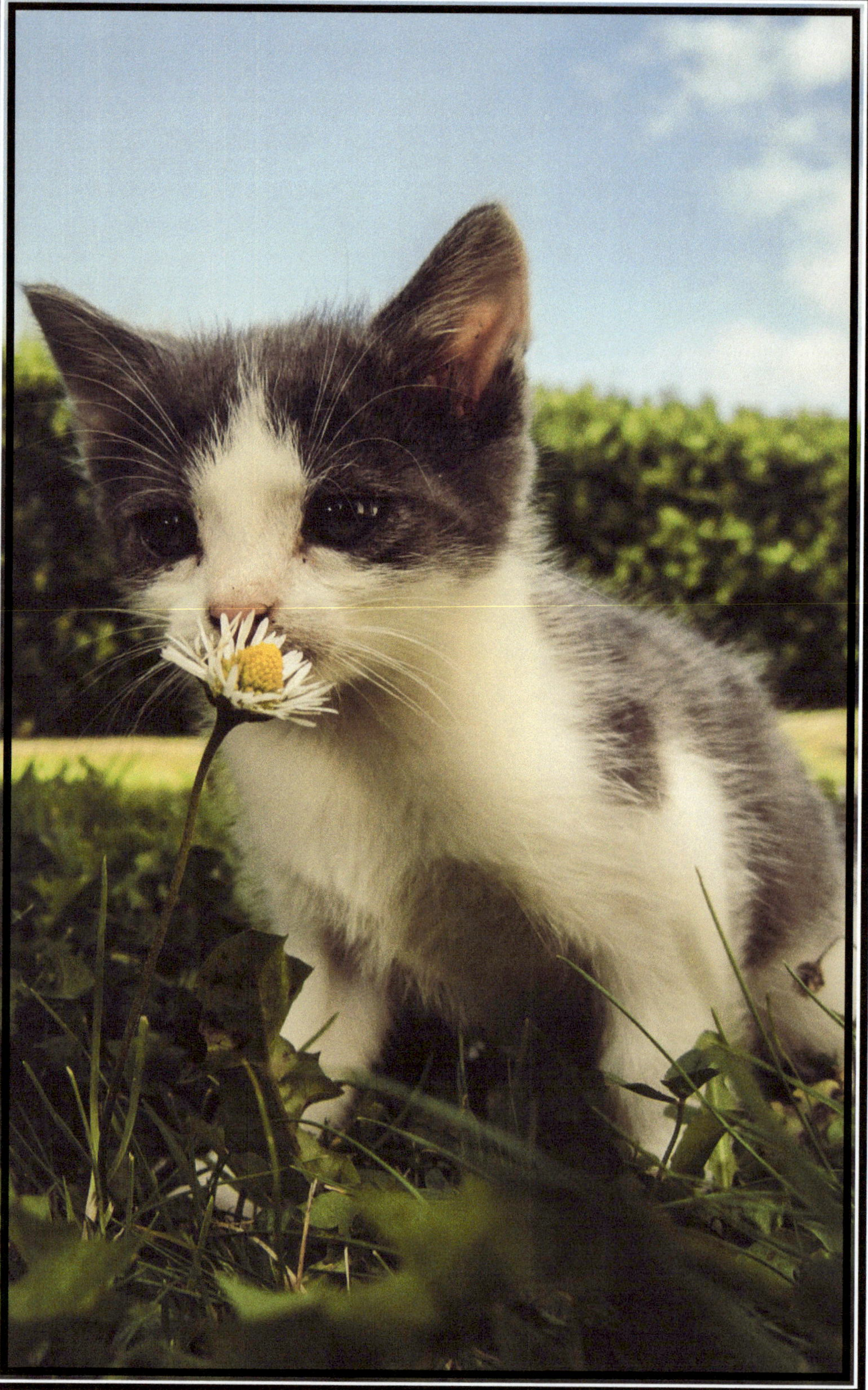

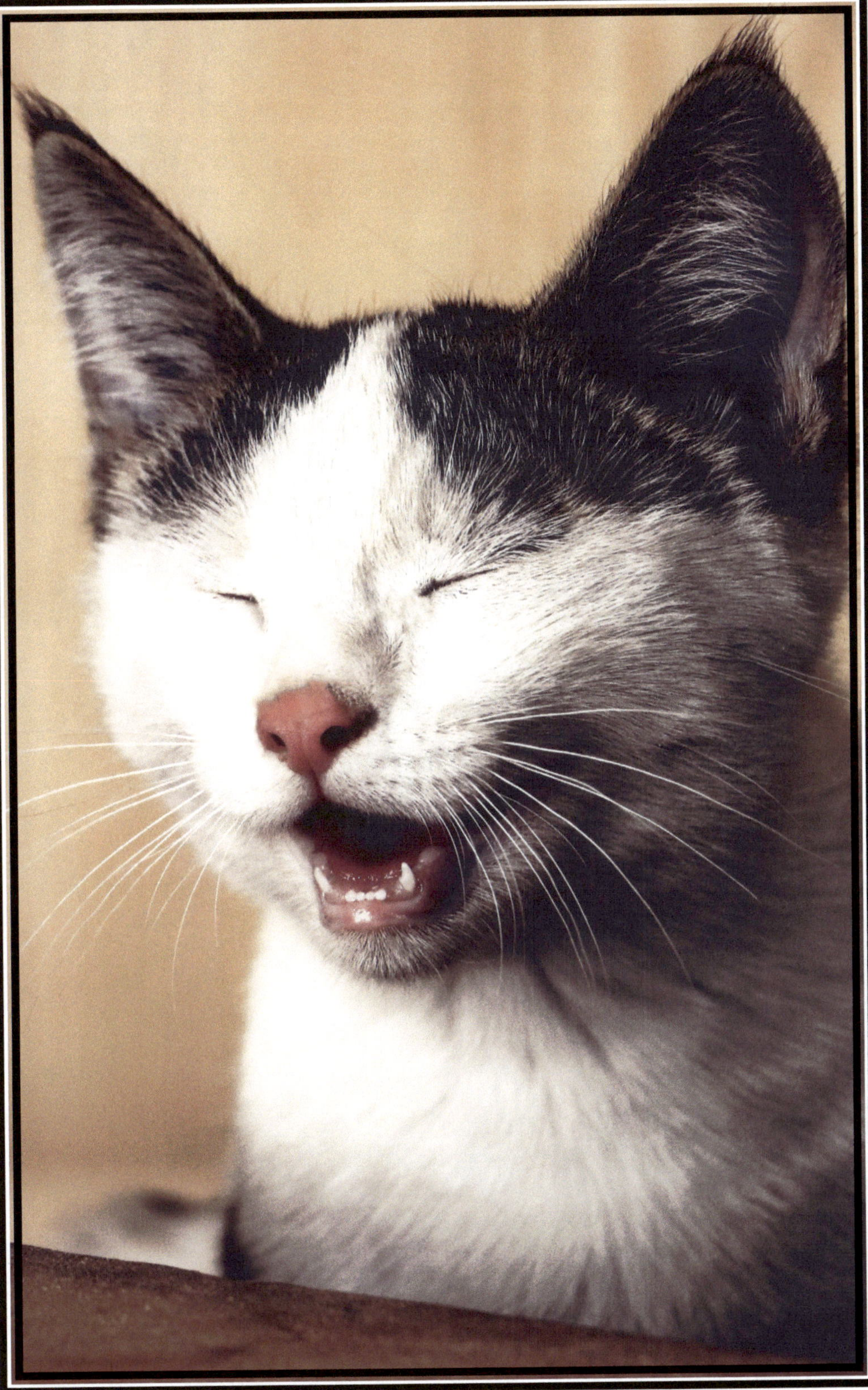

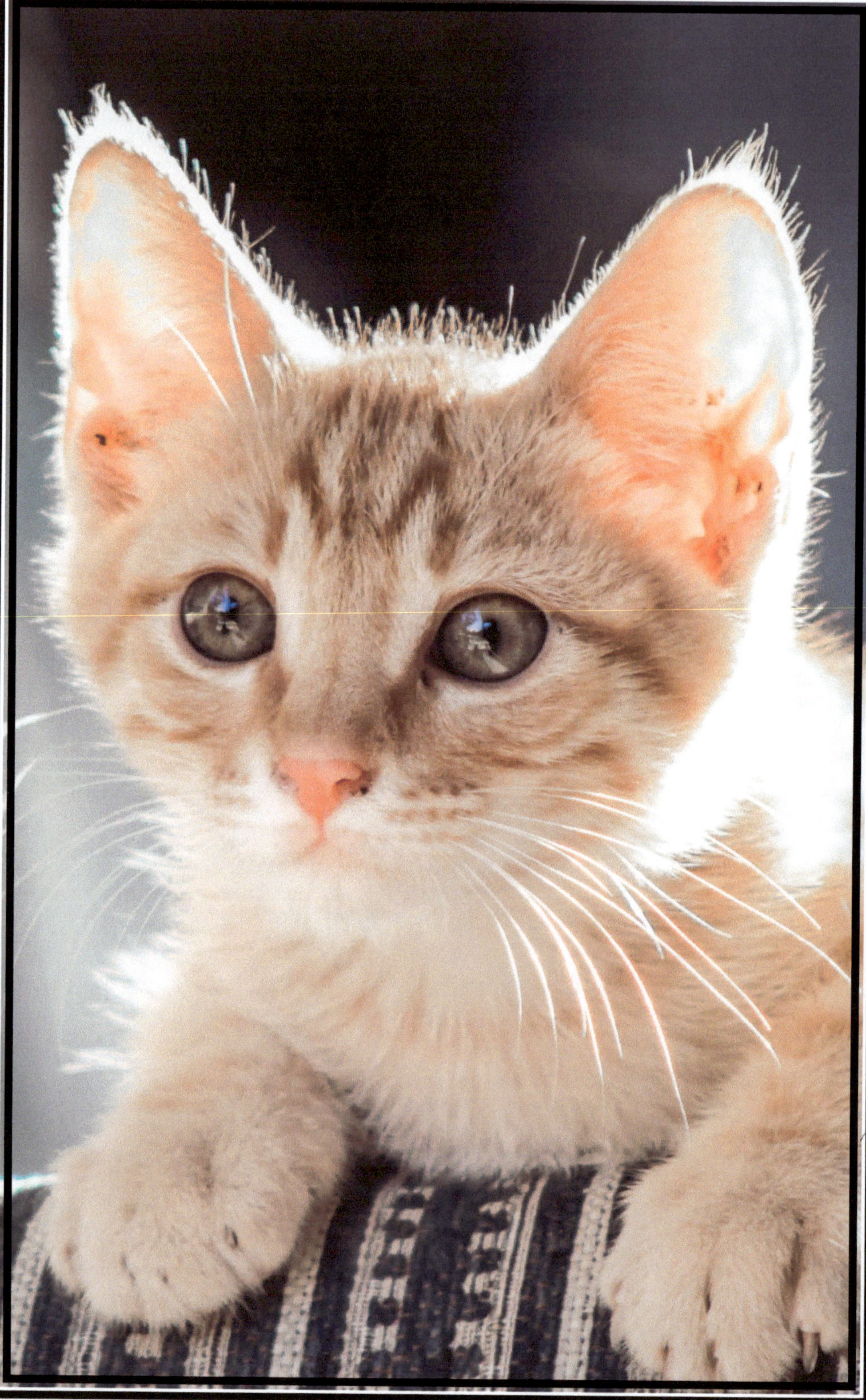

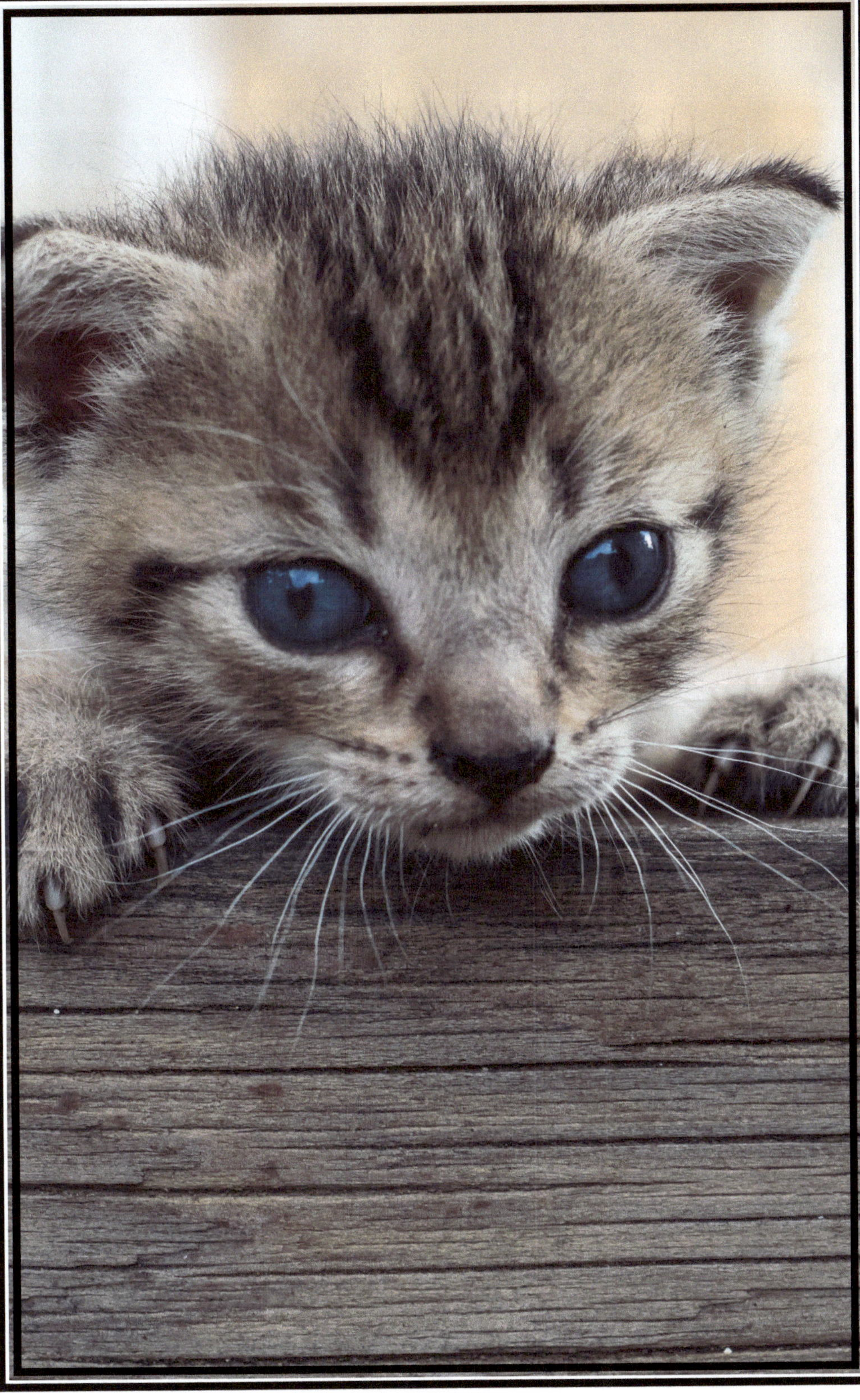

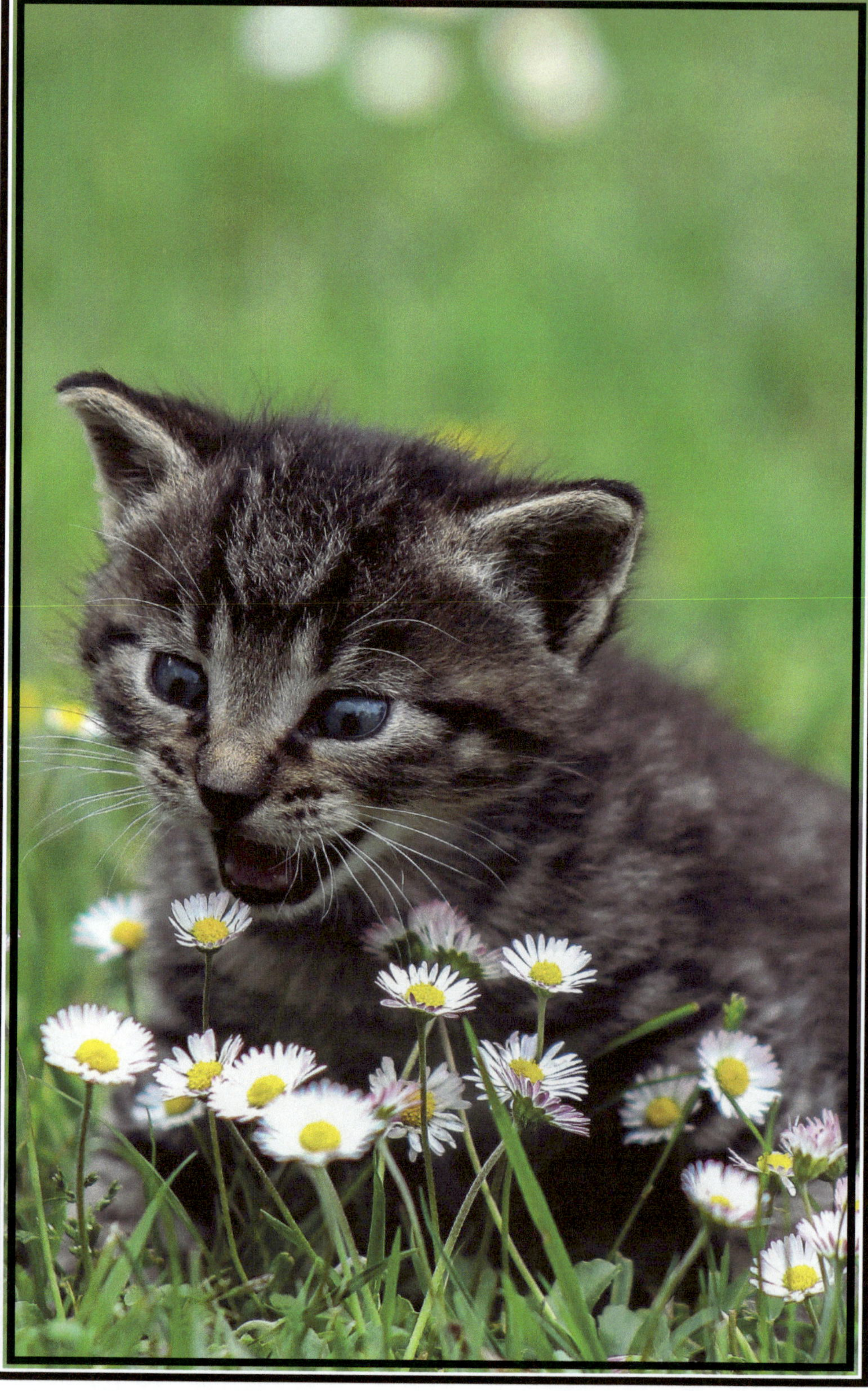

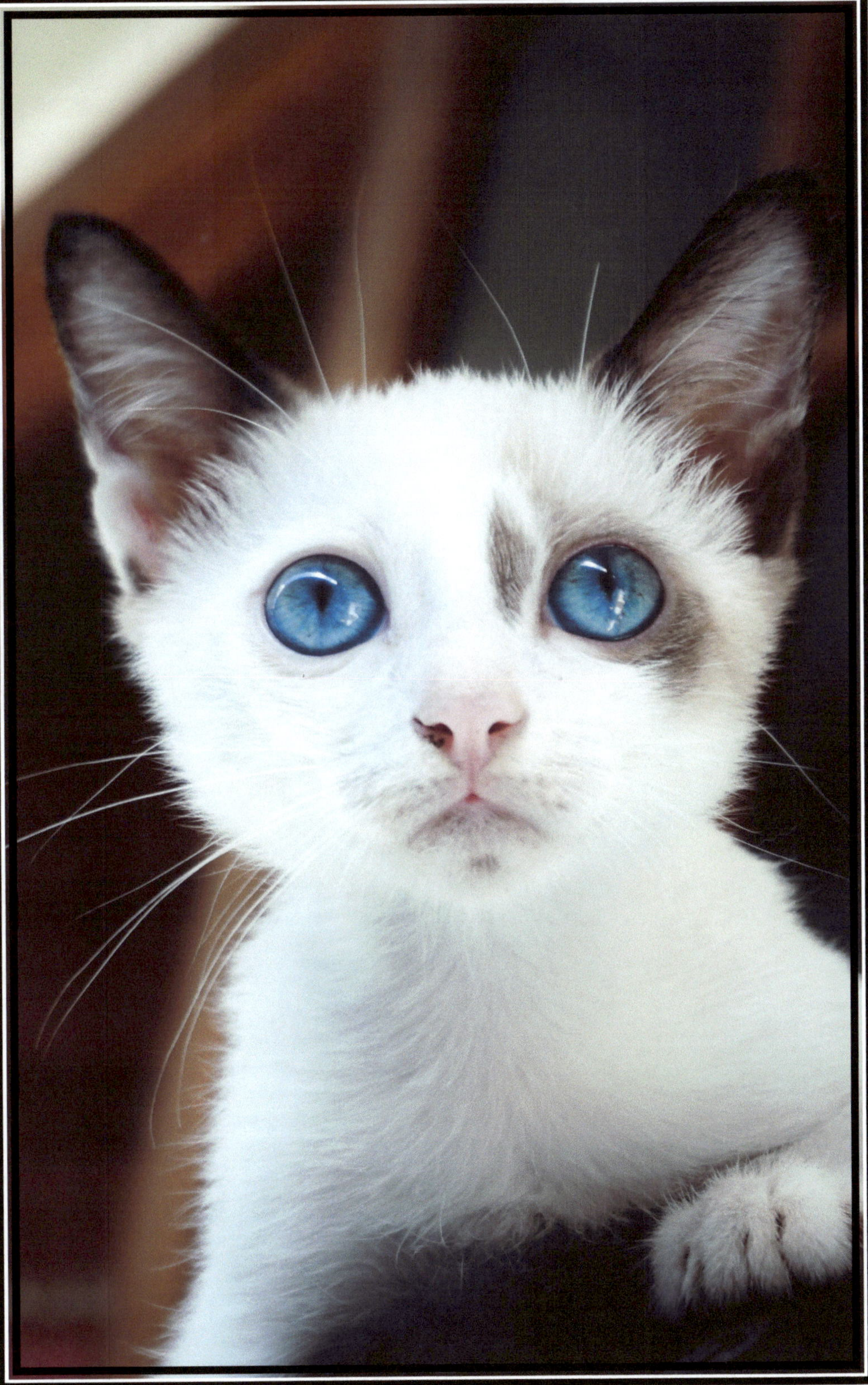

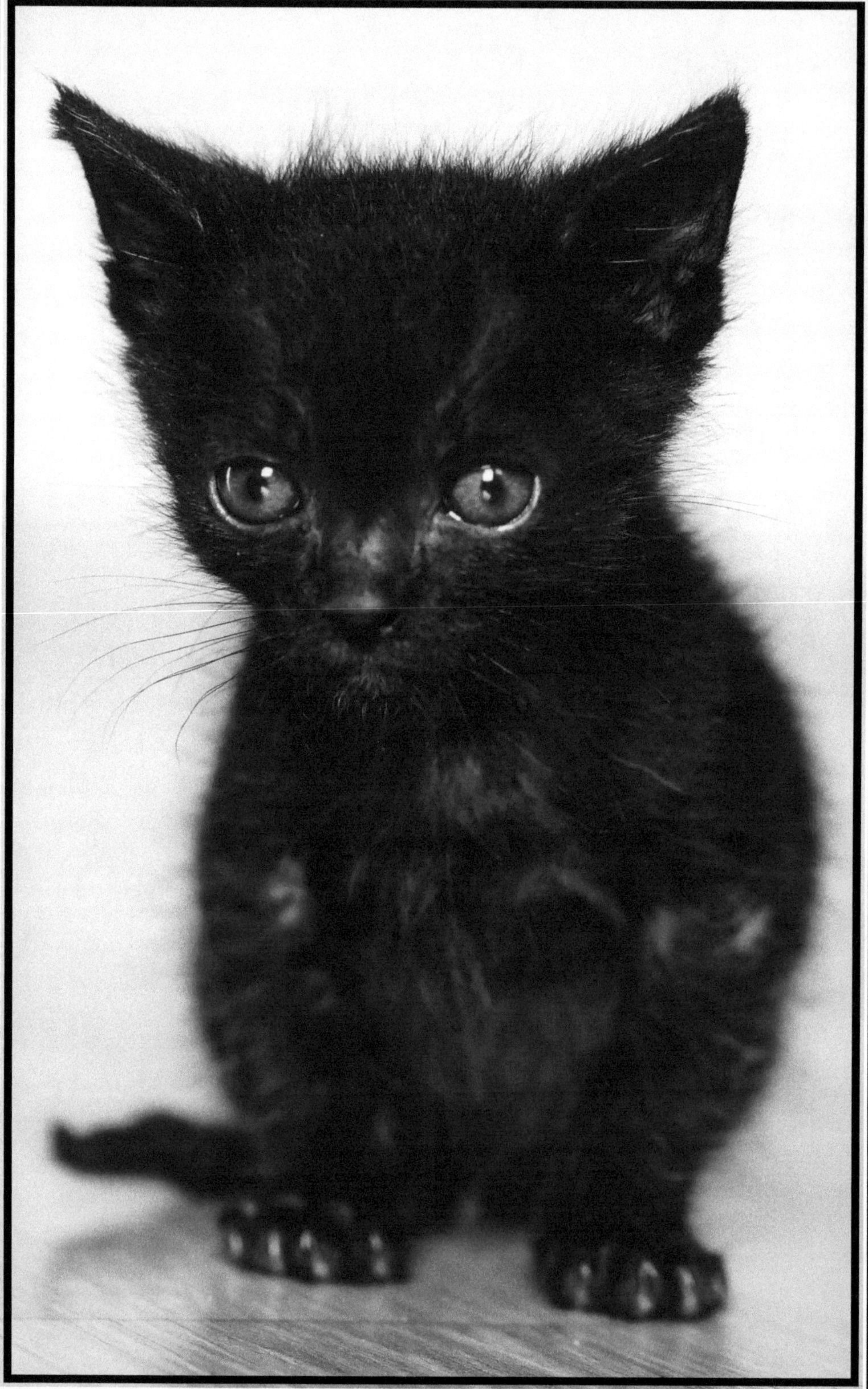

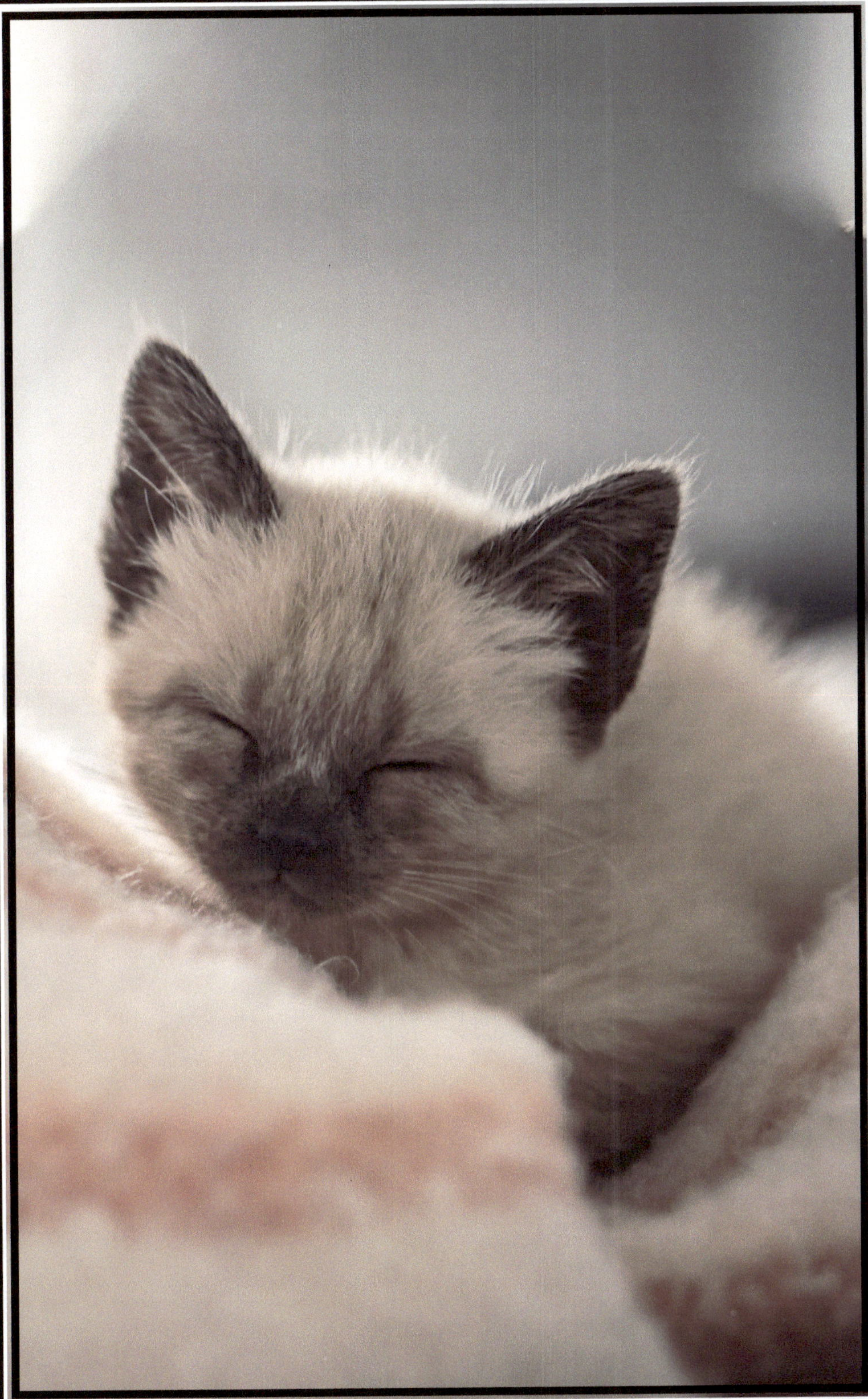

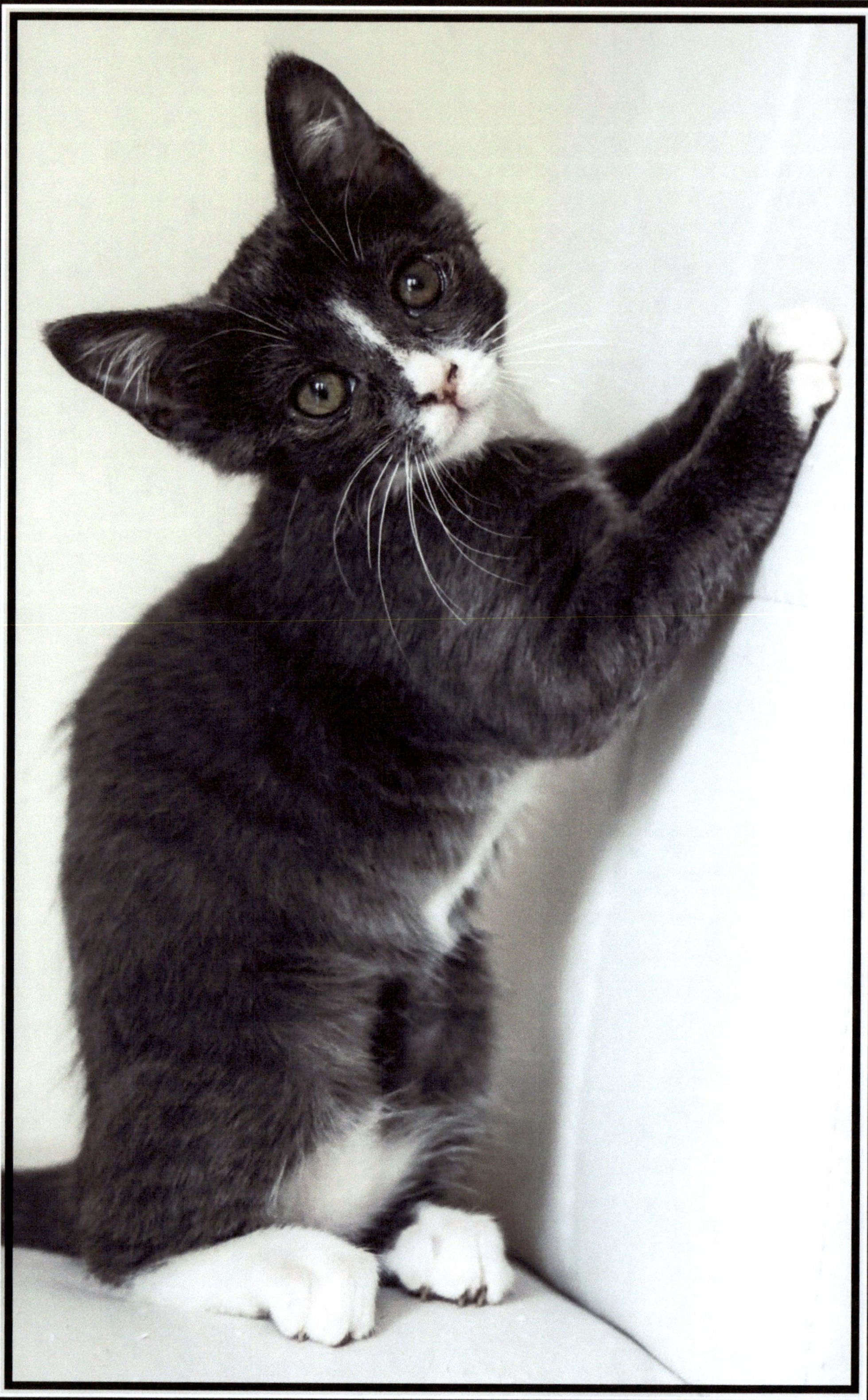

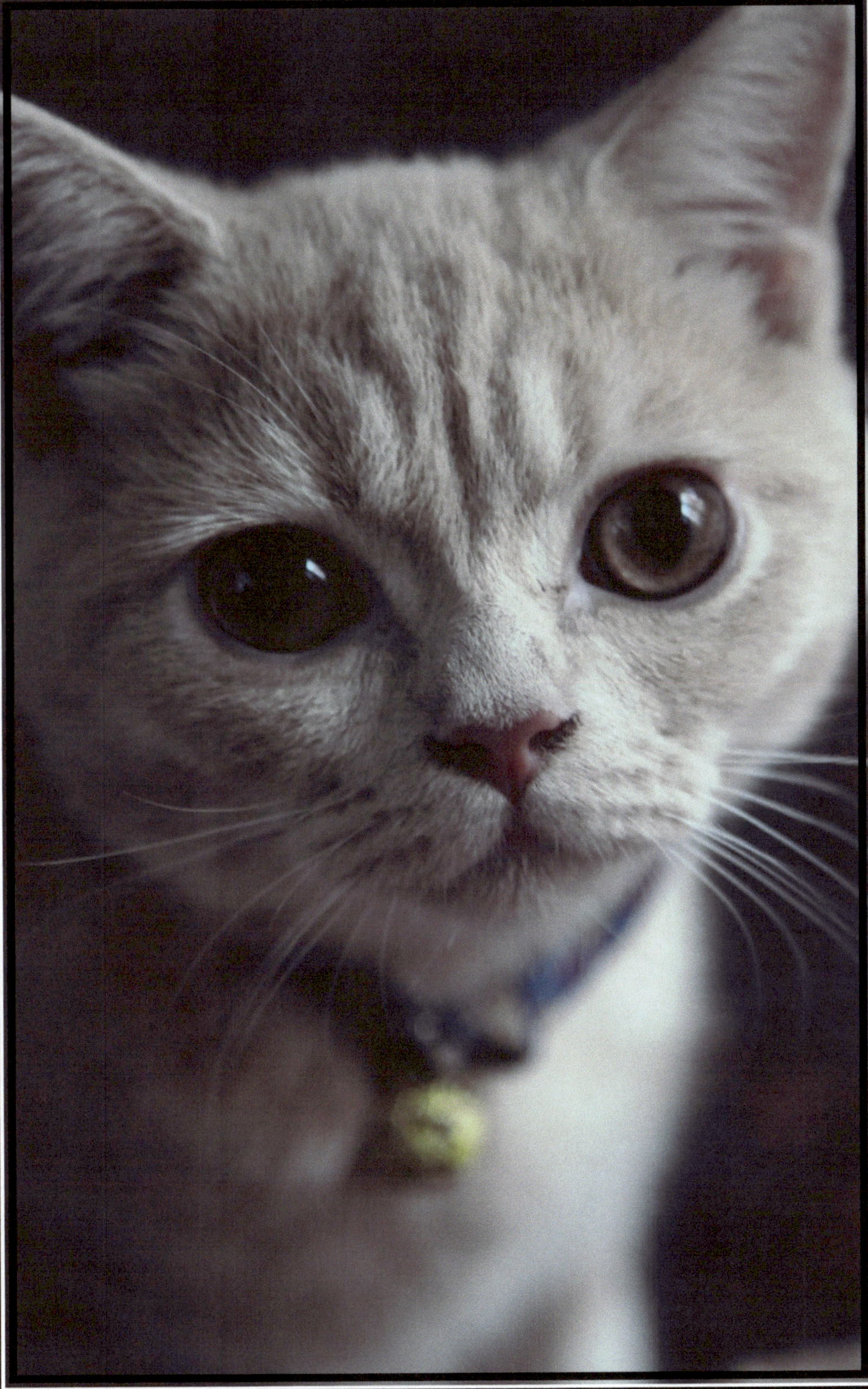

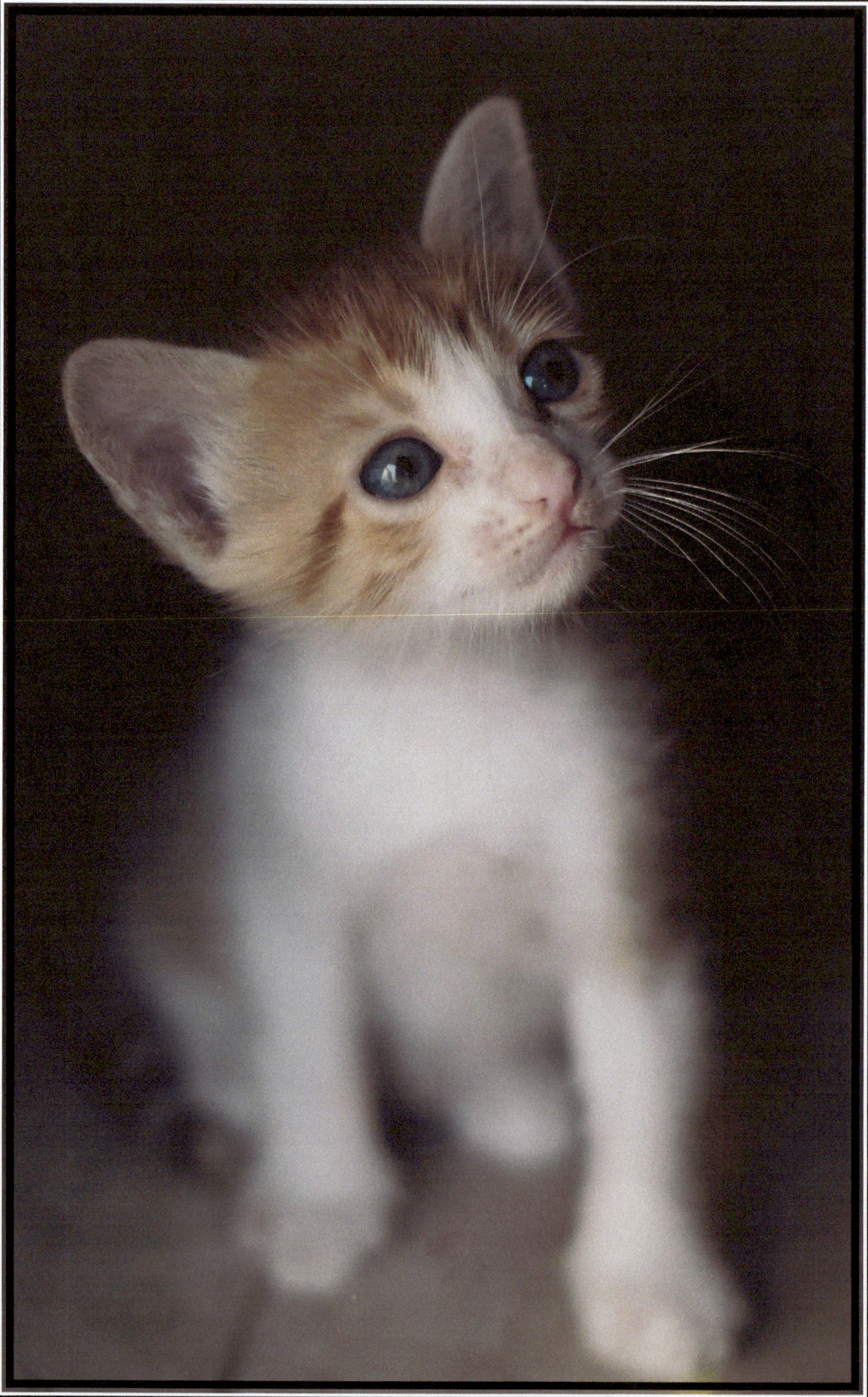

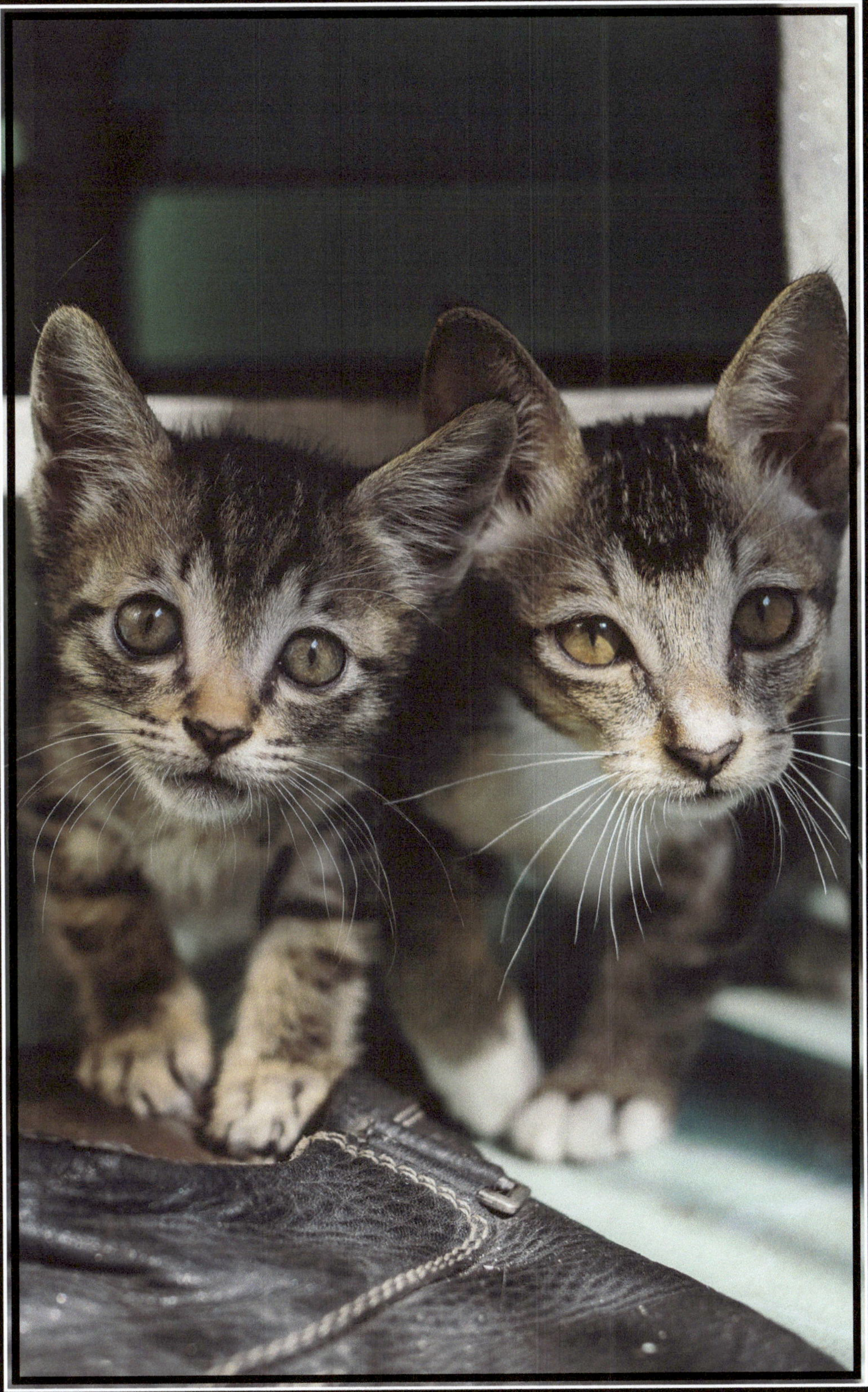

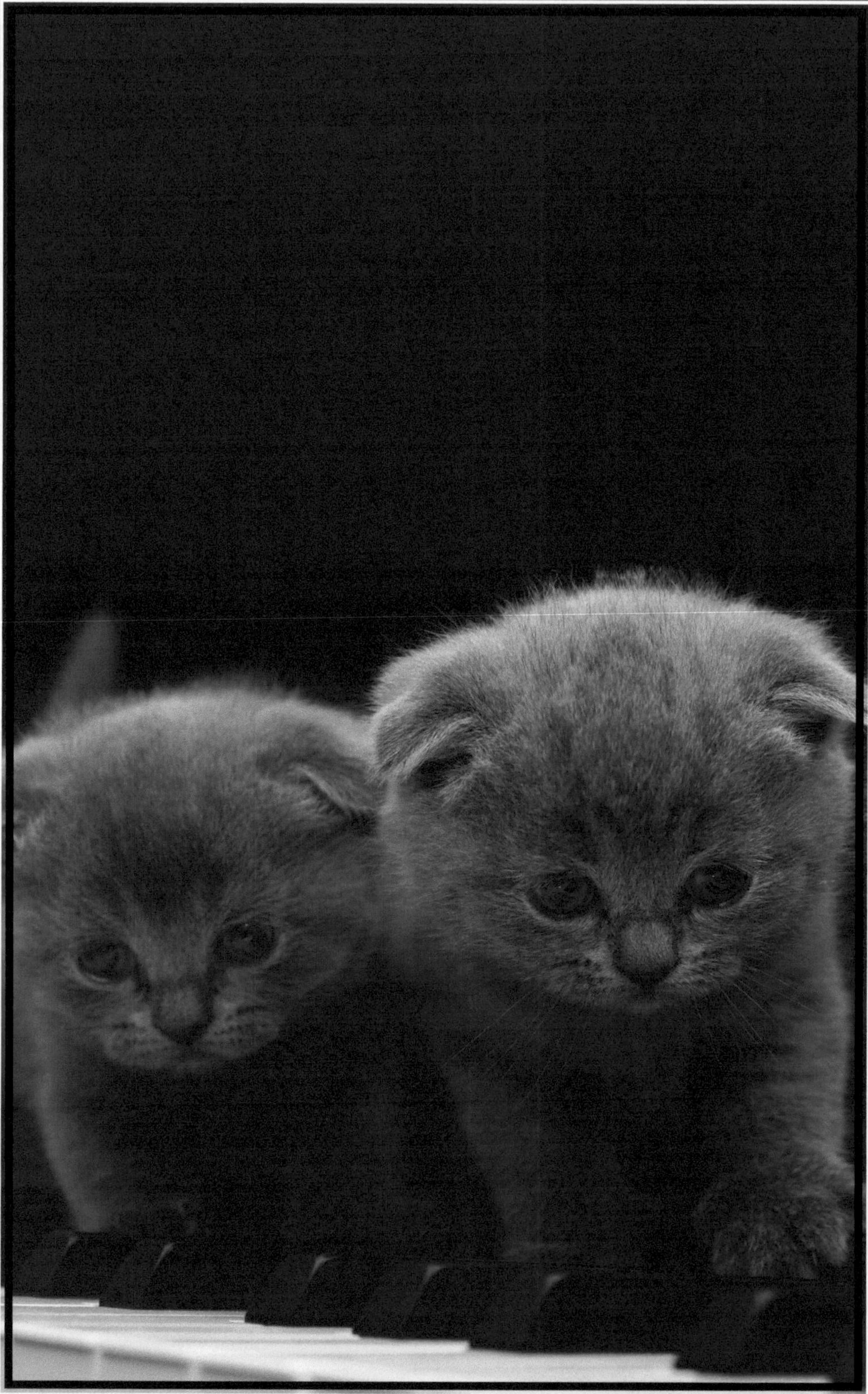

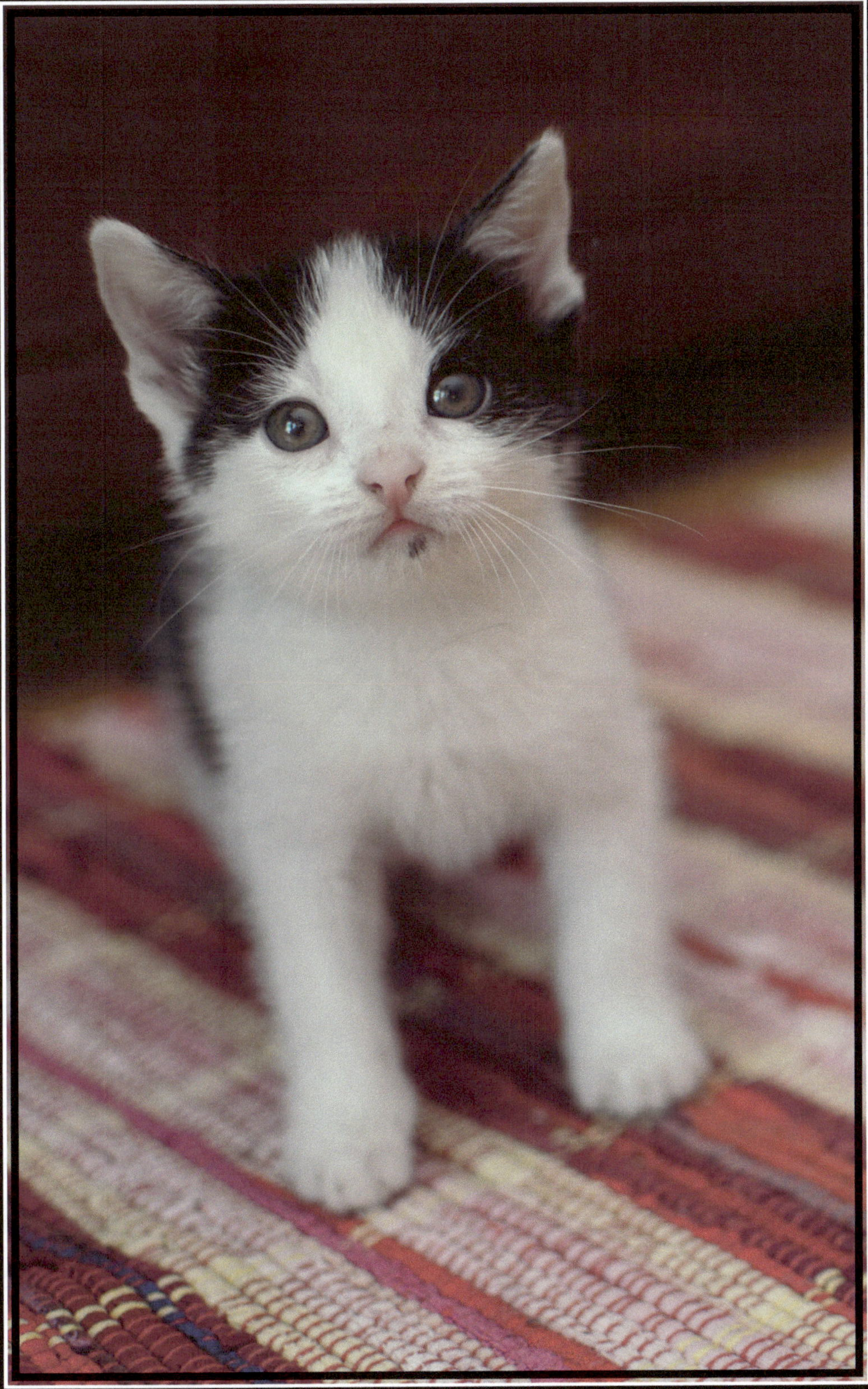

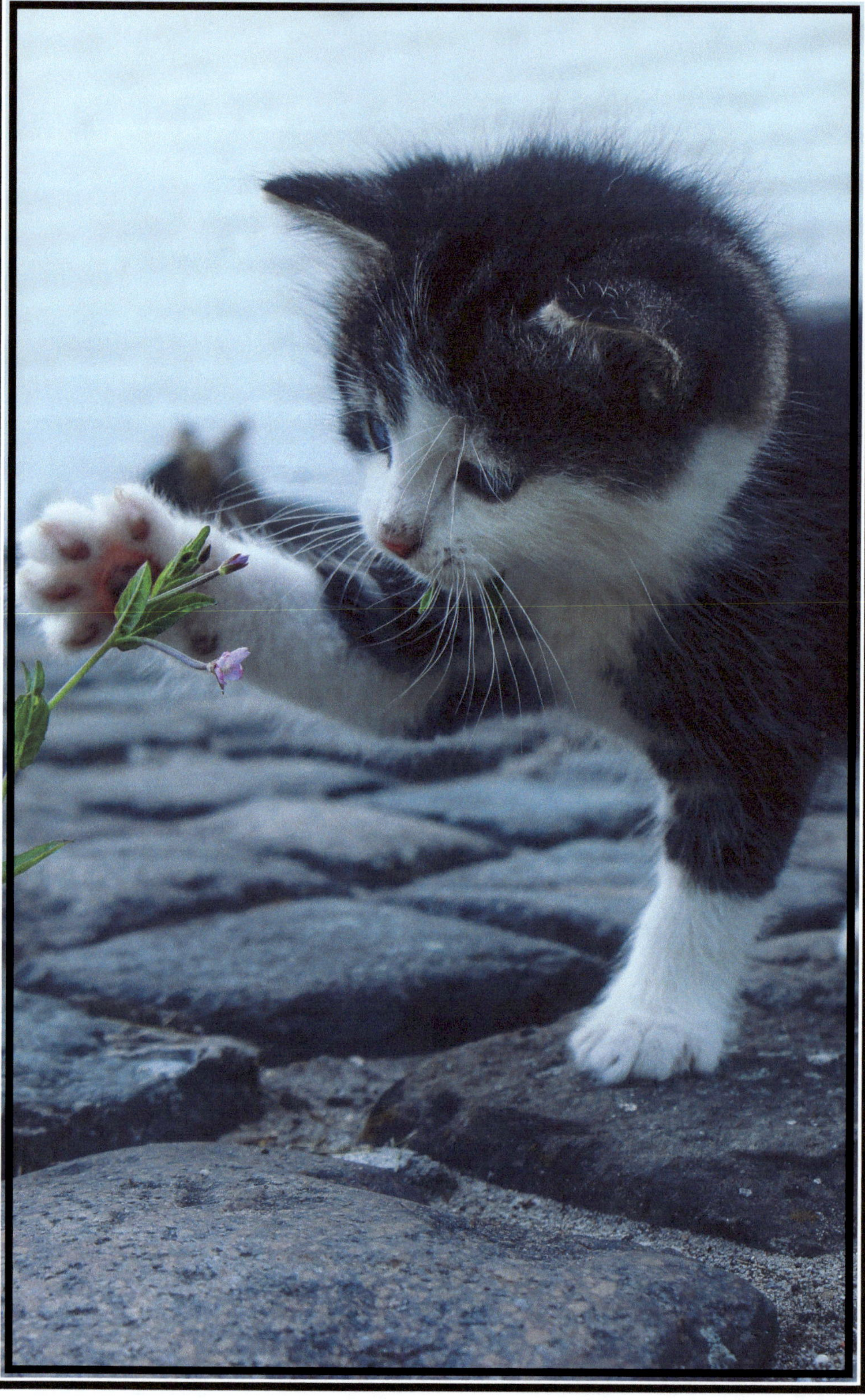

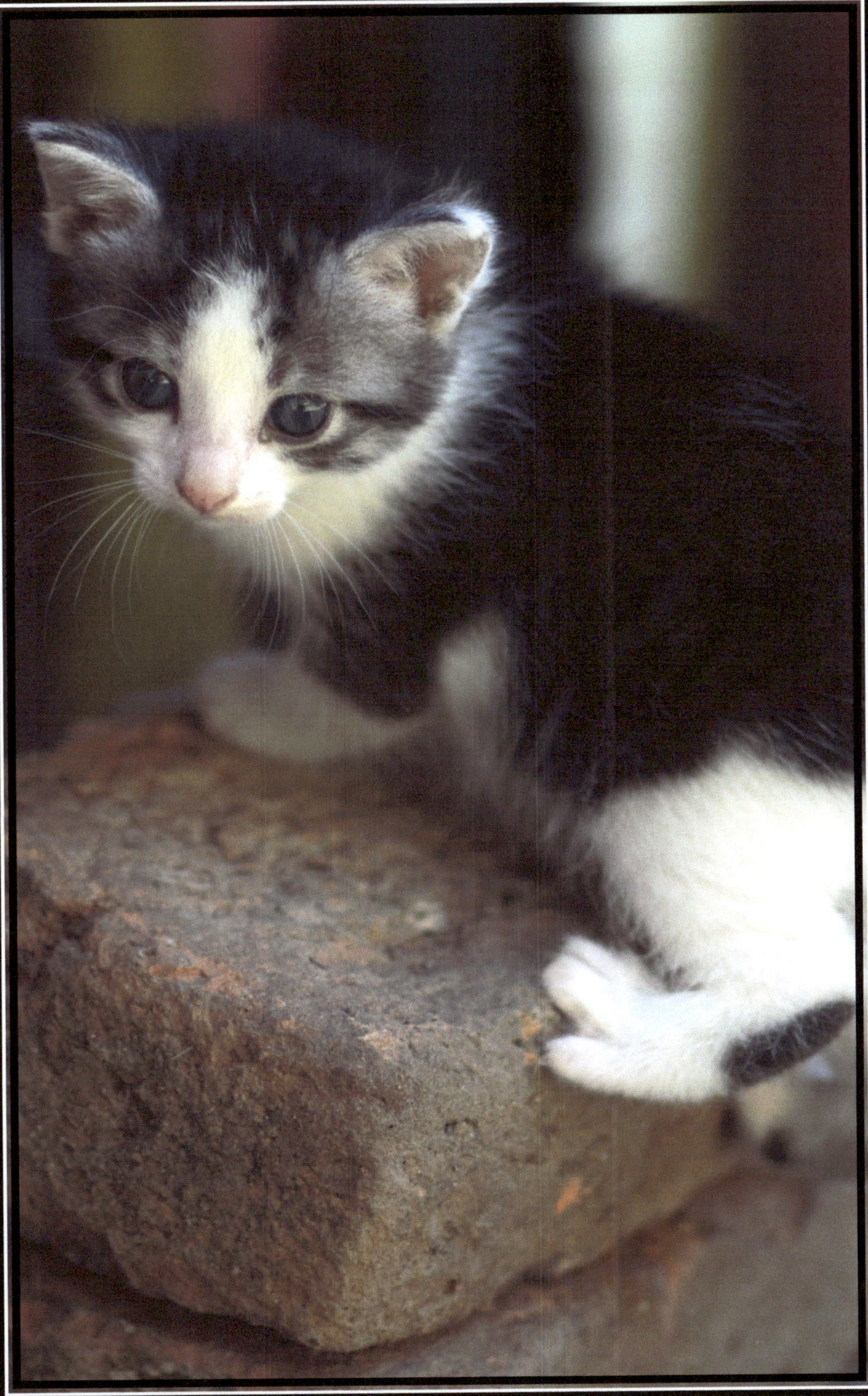

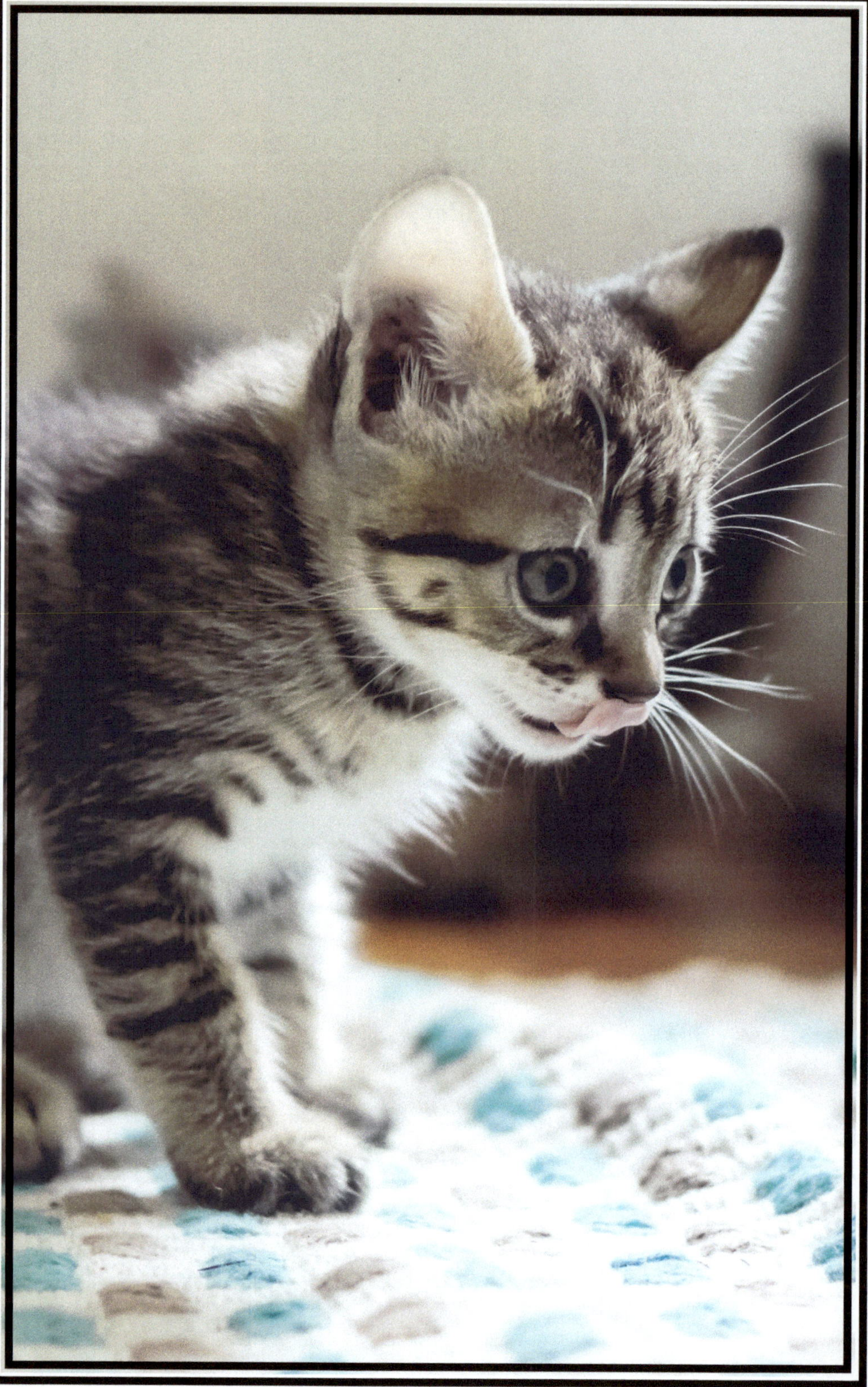

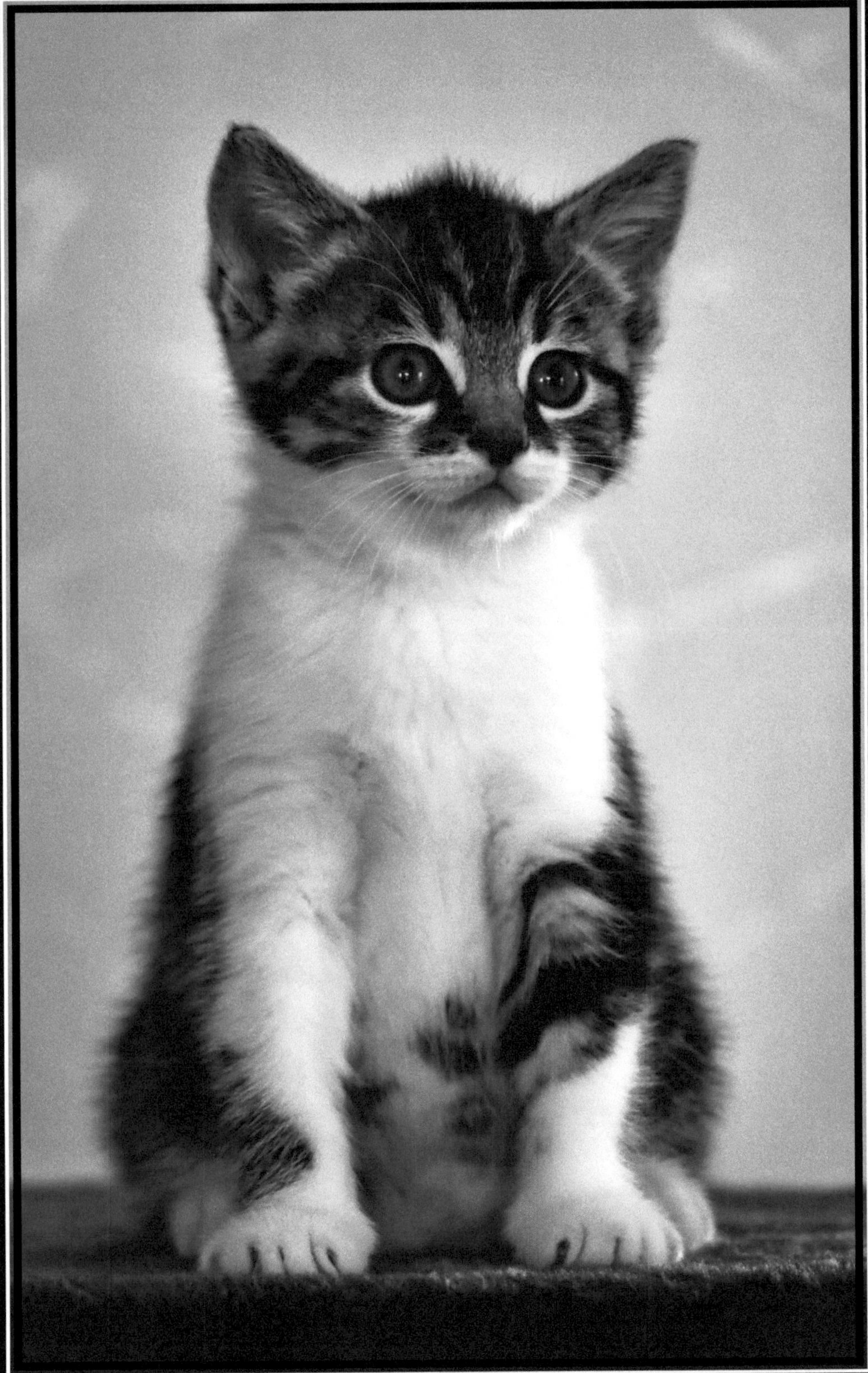